The First Ninety Days of Marriage

Eric and Leslie Ludy

W PUBLISHING GROUP
A Division of Thomas Nelson Publishers
Since 1798

www.wpublishinggroup.com

Published by W Publishing Group, a Division of Thomas Nelson, Inc., P.O. Box 141000, Nashville, Tennessee 37214. Published in association with Loyal Arts Literary Agency, www.LoyalArts.com.

W Publishing books may be purchased in bulk for educational, business, fund-raising, or sales promotional use. For information, please e-mail SpecialMarkets@ThomasNelson.com.

Scripture quotations are from the following sources: The Holy Bible, New International Version (NIV). Copyright ©1973, 1978, 1984, International Bible Society. Used by permission of Zondervan Bible Publishers; The King James Version of the Bible (KJV); The New King James Version (NKJV®), copyright 1979, 1980, 1982, Thomas Nelson, Inc., Publishers; New American Standard Bible (NASB), © 1960, 1977, 1995 by the Lockman Foundation; The Holy Bible, English Standard Version™ (ESV). Copyright © 2001 by Crossway Bibles, a division of Good News Publishers. All rights reserved.

Library of Congress Cataloging-in-Publication Data

Ludy, Eric.
    The first ninety days of marriage : laying the foundation for forever / Eric and Leslie Ludy.
      p. cm.
    ISBN 0-8499-0524-9
    1. Marriage. I. Ludy, Leslie. II. Title.
HQ734.L783 2006
248.8'44—dc22   2005036491

Printed in the United States of America
06 07 08 09 10 RRD 7 6 5 4 3 2 1

CONTENTS

AUTHOR'S NOTE

- Leslie -

Last week Eric and I attended a lovely wedding. The bride was radiant as she looked at her new husband. The groom's eyes were full of adoration as he gazed back at his bride. Their love was fresh, exciting, and full of wonder. As the crowd showered the pair with rice and best wishes, they went off into the sunset to begin their own happily-ever-after journey.

Later that same afternoon, we were in a coffee shop talking to a man who was in the midst of a bitter divorce. "I hired a private investigator and got photos of my wife cheating on me," he ranted in disgust. "So I took all of her expensive lingerie and burned it in the backyard." For five minutes he berated the woman he had once loved and committed his life to serve. He spoke about her as if she were a piece of worthless mud caked on his shoe.

Once upon a time, this man and woman had been just like the radiant young bride and groom at the wedding. This bitter couple had once gazed at each other with the same kind of love and adoration. They, too, had gone off into the sunset with hopes and dreams of happily ever after.

But, like that of all too many modern couples, their fairy tale soon began to take a nightmarish turn. Tenderness and respect were replaced with selfishness and resentment. One marital mistake piled on top of another, until suddenly one day they couldn't find anything left of the love that had brought them together in the first place.

In today's world, the idea of happily ever after can seem almost ridiculous amid heated divorce hearings, scandalous affairs, and broken homes. And yet each new bride and new groom who together walk down the aisle still dare to hope that *their* love story will be the one in a million that somehow stands the test of time.

As a newly married couple, you might have heard a common piece of advice from friends, counselors, or marriage experts. It goes something like this: "Don't let your expectations for marriage become too high. It is important to have a realistic view of what you are headed into. If you expect a fairy tale, you will be disappointed."

Yet when we are young and in love, it's hard *not* to hope for happily ever after. Despite the raging divorce epidemic, something inside us longs for more than a mediocre love story.

If you are among those who desire that "something more" for your marriage, this book was written for you. This book isn't about lowering your marriage expectations to help you avoid disappointment. This book is about *raising* your marriage expectations to help you experience a spectacular, lifelong love story. Contrary to popular opinion, Eric and I believe that fairy tales *do* exist and that happily ever after *can* be preserved for a lifetime. We believe that a successful marriage is not found when you lower your expectations. Rather, we believe that success comes when you *exchange* your human hopes and dreams for God's heavenly ones. We believe that success is a by-product of having a far loftier marriage ideal than that of the modern-day masses—*God's ideal.*

After eleven years of marriage, Eric and I can honestly say that we are more in love today than when we stood at the altar and exchanged our vows. We are living out a God-scripted fairy tale. In fact, we are a little biased, but we believe we have the most beautiful love story in the history of the world! Does that mean our marriage is without challenge and conflict? Absolutely not. But it does mean that every challenge and conflict only serves to deepen our relationship and enhance our lifelong commitment to each other. Does it mean our life has been easy? No. We have faced many intense difficulties in our journey together. But through the storms of life, our relationship is preserved and beautified, because the Author of romance is writing each chapter of our love story.

Happily ever after is impossible without the God of the universe backing you up. But when the Author of romance takes the helm, you can go off into the sunset with the utmost confidence that your fairy tale will end even more beautiful than it began. So allow yourself to dream fairy-tale dreams once again. Our hope is that this message will catapult your expectations of God-built marriage through the roof.

This book is made up of five chapters, specifically designed for your first ninety days of marriage. The first few months of your life together are when habits are formed that will affect the rest of your marriage. So we encourage you to use these precious weeks and months to lay a foundation for happily ever after.

Though some portions of this book are written to men and women individually, this is a book that is designed for you to work through together as a couple. Each chapter begins with a specific foundational principle for lifelong romance. And each chapter ends with a corresponding "Putting It into Action" section to help you practically apply that principle to your marriage right now. As you work through these "Putting It into Action" sections, you may find it helpful to use a separate notebook to record your thoughts and ideas.

We use many examples from our own marriage throughout this book to provide you with real-life illustrations of this message. But this is not done to imply that your marriage should be a replica of our own. In fact, we are confident that your relationship will be a unique testimony to God's amazing creativity and romantic flare.

Note that when we use the term *lover* in this book, we are referring to a faithful, Christ-centered spouse rather than the culture's loose and often ungodly definition of *lover*.

Also, please know that the names of some people and places

in this book have been altered in order to protect privacy (e.g., Chuck, the guy competing for the Beer Belly Hall of Fame, goes by a different name in real life!).

Eric and I are cheering you on as you go off into the sunset to start your new life together. We believe that if you make the right decisions in these early months of your marriage, you will lay the foundation for a forever kind of love. And someday, while other couples are burning each other's clothes in the backyard and hiring private investigators, you will be experiencing something altogether different. Through God's amazing grace, people will look at your life and say, "They truly lived happily ever after."

Introduction

LAYING THE FOUNDATION FOR FOREVER

> *Marriage isn't an invention of society.*
> *It's an invention of God.*

- Eric -

When my vocal coach told me that he wanted me to train for six hours every day, I let out a gasp and retorted, "Who in the world has six hours every day to work on singing?" His response shut me up quickly. "Those who want to be the best, Eric."

Having a great marriage comes down to one simple principle: those who want the best that marriage has to offer must train like Olympians to win such a golden reward. We've heard it many times: "Marriage is hard work." But when we are young and in love, most of us don't realize just how *much* effort it takes to make a marriage really work.

God intended marriage to be a little taste of heaven on earth. But the concept of a great marriage is more an *idea* nowadays than a practical reality. An amazing marriage has become merely something to dream about, not something to aim for. In modern times, we've allowed mediocrity to be our standard when it comes to marriage. We've stopped hitching our wagon to a star and allowing God to define the limits of love's potential. And many of us have stopped believing that anything better than marriage disillusionment is available. Couples in love no longer aim for the perfect marriage. The modern-day marriage mantra is simply "Let's try not to get a divorce."

What a sorry vision, or maybe I should say what a sorry *lack* of vision. If we took that same attitude into a business venture, our purpose statement would read, "Don't go bankrupt!" How inspiring is that? If this attitude were applied to a professional sports team, their chant in the huddle would be, "Don't get injured!"

God designed us to go after the impossible. He wants us to seek success, not barricade ourselves against failure. He wants us to aim for the Super Bowl, not fret about twisting an ankle along the way. This book is not about merely learning how to subsist in marriage—this book is about learning how to *thrive* in marriage. Marriage is meant to be a taste of heaven on earth, not a taste of hell on earth. Our motivation should be the heights of intimate ecstasy. *We should settle for nothing less than a perfect marriage.*

A perfect marriage, in God's design, is not without conflict or challenge. But it is a marriage in which conflict and challenge only enhance and strengthen a lifelong, God-scripted love story. A perfect marriage isn't one absent of mistakes and stumbling. Rather, it is one in which every mistake and every stumble is deemed an opportunity to become a more excellent spouse; one in which every failure only serves to inspire each of you toward ultimate success. And if you are willing to put in some focused effort, then in the next ninety days you can lay the foundation for this kind of lifelong marital bliss.

What's so important about the first ninety days of marriage? In the first three months of a new marriage, the clay is still moist and malleable. The first ninety days can define the next ninety years. If you head in the wrong direction, you end up at the wrong destination; but if you head in the right direction from the very beginning, not only are a lot of unnecessary miseries avoided, but a God-scripted destination is far easier to achieve.

In God's economy, the first ninety days of any new season of life are significant. For instance, it's during the first ninety days of pregnancy when the tiny new life is the most vulnerable and fragile. And it is in the first ninety days when a newborn is most susceptible to infection and physically vulnerable to harm. The first ninety days represent the season of supercharged development in an infant, when the greatest percentages of foundational growth take place. And like a developing new baby, a new marriage develops and grows exponentially in those first three months. It is in those first three months that the marital world is defined. The habits, both good and bad, lock into place. Roles become defined. Communication methods settle themselves in for the long haul. Sexual and emotional intimacy gets off to either the right or the wrong start.

Every couple has a choice of how they are going to begin their proverbial ride into the sunset. If the first ninety days are nonchalantly overlooked, it does not mean marital ruin. God is in the business of giving us a fresh new start *whenever* we ask Him. But if you proactively maximize your first ninety days of marriage, you will avoid years of heartache, disillusionment, and having to "unlearn" all the wrong habits that were set in those early months.

Marriage is serious business. It's intense, it's challenging— it's important work. However, we hope this book will display that marriage is also romantic, fun, and full of magical wonder. Marriage will likely be one of the hardest things you will ever do. But marriage should also be one of the most enjoyable things you ever do. Marriage is serious drama, but it's also romantic comedy. It's hilarious, it's full of wonder, and it's heartwarming. Like life itself, God made marriage to be the perfect mix of agony and ecstasy. Unfortunately, too many young couples only discover the agony and miss out on the ecstasy. But the agony is meant to help us fully experience the ecstasy and the incredible fulfillment that can be fully appreciated only by those who pass through difficulty and overcome challenge.

In the hidden alcoves of marriage, which are found only

through diligent exploration and excavation, there is unearthed a kind of pleasure and wonder that defies the bounds of human description. It is an ecstasy of such heavenly proportions that mere words are ashamed even in their attempt to define it. A scant few of today's couples ever taste this fine wine of God's vineyard. Not for lack of want, but for lack of knowledge of its very existence. If you knew nuggets of gold were buried in your backyard, you would dig for them. The same is true with this magical marriage wonder—if couples only knew it was possible to discover such depths of romantic beauty, they would seek it with all their might. But you won't dig up your backyard if you aren't confident that something precious is buried out there.

When it comes to marriage, there *is* something of divine worth waiting to be unearthed. And it is our hope that this book can serve as a map to the buried treasure; a map that will help you bring meaning to the agony of married love and acquaint you with the ecstasy of covenant intimacy.

Marriage isn't an invention of society. It's an invention of God. He brainstormed romantic intimacy and wedded bliss. He came up with the whole idea of married love. And He designed us for it. He perfectly crafted us to fit into the divinely tailored clothing of marriage and to match with the opposite of our sexual kind. He shaped us not with the intent of our sexually and emotionally depositing ourselves into a multitude of people, *but into only one.* He meant for each of us to share ourselves both inside and out with only a single individual, in the context of marriage covenant, for all our remaining days on this earth. Marriage is the perfect fit. It's not meant to be a ball and chain, but the ultimate liberation. It's a coming alive, an arousal that goes far beyond a mere physical awakening— it's an awakening of the soul. And to many of us who think of God as having a fun phobia, it is strange to realize that this awakening is good, pure, noble, extraordinarily pleasure-filled, *and actually endorsed and encouraged by the Almighty God of the universe.*

God is a huge fan of marriage because He knows what marriage can do to build men and women into marvelous examples of His nature. Sure, marriage can, if not used correctly, make a selfish person more selfish. But if marriage is used as God intended, it is a factory for the production of selfless servanthood. It's a training ground for divine service, the of washing another's feet, and extreme sensitivity. It's a training ground for perseverance, loyalty, protectiveness, intimacy, and loving communication. Marriage, when done right, is an extraordinary enhancement to the human life. It is a launchpad into a whole new dimension of growth with God.

God never intended marriage to be a drudgery. He designed it to be a foretaste of heaven. He didn't craft it to start with fireworks and go out with fading smoke. Much to the contrary, He crafted it to start with fireworks and turn into the aurora borealis—a glorious display of His supernatural love and grace. In God's economy, marriage is supposed to get better and better with time—not the other way around.

For your marriage to work, you need the right attitude, the

right expectations, and the right tools. And that is what this book is about. It's about learning the basics to make a forever kind of love a reality in your newborn covenant relationship.

It is our hope that this book will both inspire you and equip you to fully enjoy this first season of your new life together as a couple. Please excuse us if we come across as a little too excited about the truths in this book. Leslie and I love married life! As Leslie mentioned earlier, after more than eleven years of marriage, we can attest that it only gets sweeter and sweeter as time passes. It is our hope that you can share in the same overwhelming joys the two of us experience on a daily basis.

Here's to happily ever after!

Chapter One

HOW TO HAVE
THE PERFECT MARRIAGE

> *Great marriages aren't stumbled upon;*
> *they are fought for.*

- Eric -

I woke up this morning, as I do every morning, with the desire to have the greatest marriage in the history of the world. Aiming to have the perfect marriage is my mission; it's my quest; it's my Mount Everest. And yes, I'm fully aware of how great my quest is.

Where others aim to become the world's fastest human or the next American Idol, my ambition is a bit misunderstood by the mainstream mentality. I know great marriage doesn't come cheap—I know how much such a lofty ambition will cost me. It will take my pride and flush it down the toilet; it will tax every millimeter of my soul and ruthlessly expose my every selfish tendency; it will renovate my entire existence.

And I say, "Bring it on!"

A great marriage is like an Olympic event. To compete at

a world-class level in the arena of love demands extreme dedication, the focus of your entire being, and a staggering expenditure of heart, mind, and body. Marriage is certainly not life under a shade tree—it's an emotional, physical, and psychological obstacle course in which only the fortified survive. Great marriages are the stuff of the heartiest and stoutest souls. Marriage inevitably weeds out the serious lovers from the casual holidayers seeking a short-term thrill and a few wedding gifts. Marriage is boot camp for the soul, the testing of the fiber of the heart, and the proving ground for the true substance of one's love.

And I say, "Bring it on!"

Great marriages aren't stumbled upon; they are fought for. And if you achieve this impossible goal, there is no gold medal awaiting you on a podium in the end, no screaming crowd to applaud your many efforts, and no Wheaties-box photo op to authenticate your sacrifice for posterity. No one outside your God, your spouse, and your children may ever know what you have achieved.

And I say, "Bring it on!"

Great marriage garners a much greater reward than mere human accolades. It wins the applause of heaven, the utter delight and total affection of your spouse for a lifetime, the purest and most perfect intimate pleasure a human can possibly know, and as a final bonus, the lifelong admiration and respect of your children. A great marriage may cost you everything, but it also will unlock your heart to know the depths of the Lord Almighty. In short, a great marriage gives back ten thousand times more than it takes.

So I say, "Bring it on!"

What did you wake up this morning desiring to pursue? A cup of Starbucks coffee? A few more hours of sleep? An available bathroom? In the first ninety days of your new life together as a couple, you have an opportunity to establish a larger vision for your life as newlyweds. You, too, can share in my wake-up routine, desiring to make *your* marriage into the world's very best. In fact, it's my desire that you will enter into a little bit of healthy competition with me and say, "Eric, your love story with Leslie is not even going to compare to mine!" As Paul encouraged the Romans, "Outdo one another in showing honor" (Rom. 12:10 ESV). I want you to look at my desire as a threat. I want your competitive juices to flow, and I want your heart to burn with a clear sense of purpose. I want you to give me a run for my money! I want you to try to "outdo" me. After all, what's the challenge in it if no one else tries? Imagine God saying to me, "Well, Eric, you're the only one who even attempted, so I guess you are the champion." That's no fun! When I was eleven I won a huge trophy at a piano competition, but it was because I was the only contestant. Believe me, there's no satisfaction in winning that way!

What sort of marriage are you going to aim for? A miserable one? A mediocre one? Or a marvelous one? Should I consider you serious competition or just another signer of a marriage license?

This book is about having a marvelous marriage—a marriage that sparkles, a marriage that will go the distance without ever losing its luster, a marriage that makes Hollywood's rendition of romance look forlorn and in need of a makeover. This book is written for those who are willing to do whatever it takes to scale the Mount Everest of married love. This book is for those willing to wake up every morning and compete with Leslie and me for the world championship of lifelong romance.

If you are in, then you need to be *all* in. Olympians train six to eight hours a day to gain mastery of their craft. What are you willing to give to gain mastery in marriage? Are you willing to put in the time, the effort, and the passion necessary to do it right? If you only want to offer your spouse a peck on the cheek as you leave for work each morning and roses once a year on Valentine's Day, this book isn't for you. But if you want to train like a champion, taste the mind-boggling ecstasy of marriage intimacy, and share in the most perfect satisfaction this side of heaven, then read on.

Superhero Secrets

Since I was a little tike, I've wanted to have big muscles. But no matter how hard I've tried, it just hasn't worked out for me. I seem to have a body that refuses to look cool. As a result of this muscle fetish, you can probably understand why my childhood heroes were Samson, Superman, Arnold Schwarzenneger, the Bionic Man, and Popeye the Sailor Man. But I realized as I grew older that each one of these men had a secret to their strength that made it difficult, if not impossible, for me to imitate. Samson had the Nazirite vow and the long hair thing going on, Superman was from another planet, Arnold worked out with weights six hours a day, the Bionic Man had to have six million dollars' worth of surgery, and, of course, Popeye had to eat spinach. Why couldn't superheroes just eat Pop-Tarts, wear Levi's, and listen to Bon Jovi? Why did they have to be so extreme, so different? Why did their secret have to be something so difficult to apply in my own life?

As humans, it's tempting to seek the easy way to the top. We want to make our millions in the lottery, build our muscles with steroids, find instant fame through a reality show, and become well-read with Cliffs Notes. Most of us don't want to travel the real road to success—the one that involves hard work and sacrifices. Not many of us are willing to take a Nazirite vow and look like a fool to the world around us, live life as if we are from another planet, spend the juiciest hours of every day in training, yield ourselves to God's operating knife, and worst of all, swallow our spinach to gain superhuman strength. But such is the map to real marriage success.

Are you willing to take your spinach? If so, I'd like to introduce you to the two secrets of all great spouses. I assure you they won't seem very appealing on the outside; superhero secrets never do. But if you are willing to take a Nazirite-like vow and go under God's surgical knife, you, too, could become the next superhero spouse.

Superhero Secret #1: Going Under God's Surgical Knife

Superhero spouses are those who learn to love out of a heavenly implanted heart.

The other day I had a conversation with a young married man at the local coffee shop. We'll call him Barry. Like many other young men his age, Barry is an aficionado of marriage mediocrity.

"It's nag, nag, nag!" he said a little louder than was socially appropriate for conversation in a public place. His lip snarled in disgust as he took a long sip from his Starbucks beverage. "My wife wants me to be something I'm just not!"

I let Barry rage on for several minutes, providing me with a few more quotations for this book. "I just tell her, look, babe, you need to stop trying to make our marriage into a fairy tale—that just isn't reality." My favorite was Barry's description of what really makes a marriage work. "When she finally gives up trying to turn me into her personal Prince Charming, then we might just get somewhere!"

When Barry finally awakened to the fact that he'd been talking for five minutes straight without even asking me a question, he turned the conversation in my direction.

"So, man, what type of work do you do?"

"Oh, I'm a writer."

"That's cool, man!" he said. "What do you write about?"

"Romance and relationships."

After that, Barry began shuffling around awkwardly and quickly changed the subject to the poor job the electrician did in installing the electrical outlet on the coffee shop wall.

It's fairly obvious that Barry is no superhero spouse. But then, let's be honest, none of us are. The problem with Barry isn't found in the fact that he is not a Prince Charming; it's the fact that he doesn't believe he can ever even become one. He lacks both vision and willingness. He has bought into the "I'm a guy and this is the way I'm always gonna be!" syndrome. That syndrome spells the end of every potential superhero husband. And the problem doesn't just lie with guys. Women frequently buy into a similar mind-set, sabotaging their ability to become superhero wives.

The ability to love well, unfortunately, doesn't come naturally to anyone. But there are two ways of looking at the "Barry" tendency in all of us. One is to say, "This is just the way I am, so learn to live with it, babe!" But the second option, though odd and uncomfortable, breeds superhuman results. It simply says, "I don't have what it takes in and of myself to be a great spouse. I need something more! And, babe, because I love you so much, I'll go under the operating knife to get it!"

Imagine how Popeye must have felt when he heard that his great strength could be gained only through endless jars of spinach. You may very well feel an identical nauseating reflex in the back of your throat when you realize that amazing spouses find their strength in . . . ahem . . . *giving up their lives.* Popeye actually had it pretty easy when you consider what God truly requires of those of us who want to be great spouses. Remember, superhero secrets never sound very appealing, and that's why there are only a few in each generation willing to don the red cape of greatness.

The Bionic Man had to die before he was brought back to life as a superhero. He lay lifeless on the operating table while the government decided to invest six million dollars' worth of biotechnology into his hapless body. He had to go under the surgical knife. Large pieces of him had to be removed before the cool superhuman gadgets could be placed within him. He woke up a different man. He woke up on that operating table as a man able to pull off the impossible.

The Bionic Man is but a pitiful shadow of what God desires to do in and through us if we will simply give up our lives and submit to His operating table. Great lovers are not made through grit, determination, and romantic sentiment. Great lovers are the creations of a heavenly surgeon. If we let go of our lives as we now know them and allow Him to take us under the knife, He doesn't invest a mere six million dollars' worth of biotechnology in us. Rather, He surgically plants His heart, His mind, His vision, His love, His joy, His peace, His strength, and His passion into our being. He pulls off a medical miracle and surgically places His very own life inside our skin. And when we wake up, we wake up different people. We wake up on His operating table as people able to pull off the impossible. We are then able to live and love like the ultimate superhero named Jesus Christ. Because it is no longer we who are living, but Christ who is living in us (see Galatians 2:20).

We all desire the perfect marriage. Even those of us who relate to Barry would love to share in a marriage that sparkles with endless pleasures. We all long for the stuff that great fairy tales are made of, growing old and gray next to one we fall more and more in love with as the years go by. But the perfect marriage is impossible for any of us attempting to do it by human effort. The perfect marriage is possible only if we yield to the superheroic life of God and allow Him to love in and through us.

To give up your life and submit to God's operating table will be possibly the hardest thing you may ever do while living on planet Earth. Every instinct in your being will scream, "Don't let go of the controls!" When it comes to "dying to self," the Barry tendency in each of us barks loudly in protest. But superhero spouses are those who learn to love out of a heavenly implanted heart. So I encourage you to seriously consider going under God's surgical knife and giving up the controls of your life. Yes, it's a painful operation, but trust me, the results are divine.

Superhero Secret #2: Training Like an Action Hero

The secret to becoming the ultimate lover is to cultivate the life of the heavenly Lover within.

Jed has a pile of fluffy brown hair atop his head, and, like me, has a body much more suited for golf than football. Well-meaning women refer to him as "skinny," though to him, the word *skinny* is derogatory. But despite his unwieldy hairdo and his supremely thin frame, Jed is quite a skilled love technician. In fact, in his premarriage relationship with Meri, who is now his wife, he proved himself more than worthy of the title "Hopeless Romantic."

He literally swept Meri off her feet the day he proposed, donning a white prince costume and riding a white horse. His poetic flare combined with his creative genius won Meri's heart, as she says, "a hundred times over." Jed's specialty was flowers. Every flower that he gave Meri was accompanied with a poetic definition of what that flower would always represent in their life together. He was a gentleman, a protector, and a sensitive student of the one he loved. Jed's romantic fervor deeply impacted Meri, and she couldn't wait to spend her life with such a thoughtful and creative man.

Unfortunately, Jed lost the magic once the honeymoon was over. He just couldn't whip up the romance, the poetic thoughts just weren't there anymore, and the flower idea was too expensive to keep up on a gym teacher's salary. After three months of Meri's cooking, Jed also claimed that he no longer fit into the white prince costume either.

"I promised Meri before we were married," Jed confided in me, "that I wouldn't ever become like one of those sedentary Barcalounger husbands who let the romance slip away once the honeymoon ended."

Jed is so frustrated with himself. He pulled off some incredible romantic stunts while winning Meri's heart. But little did Jed realize that romancing a girl's heart in the premarriage years is completely different from romancing a wife's heart for a lifetime thereafter. It's important to note that Jed isn't like Barry (mentioned in the previous section), who doesn't even desire to be a Prince Charming for his girl. Jed really does want to be a superhero in his home.

"Living with a woman is a lot harder than I expected," Jed confessed. "I lose my patience so easily with Meri. Even though I want to be sensitive and loving, for some reason I am constantly saying things I regret."

As Jed is realizing, marriage demands more out of us than we are able to give. It calls for something superhuman. And Jed is feeling it. Ordinary, romantically inclined Jed is not strong enough to lift the thirteen-ton barbell that marriage throws at us, chuckling and saying, "Go ahead and try to lift me. I dare you!"

Jed realizes that he desperately needs God's help to make his marriage work but doesn't know how exactly God would want to help him. And this is where secret #2 comes in.

God wants to take Jed—and all of us who are willing— through superhero boot camp.

When God surgically implants Himself into a human body,

His superhero development has only just begun. He wants men like Jed to know that He doesn't make great spouses overnight. Instead, He crafts them over time. He trains them like athletes. He builds them like action heroes.

Think of how strange and extraordinary this is. If Jed yields to the God of the universe and allows Him to have His way in his life, then a superheroic new life will be active and alive within his human skin. That's a bit Marvel-Comics-strange, don't you think? But what is even more strange and extraordinary is how this life actually will grow and coordinate itself within his life, taking over every facet, every corner of his existence until it is perfectly integrated into every action of his every day and into every part of his relationship with Meri.

Although Jed has always been the one in control of his actions, after this surgical invasion of Jed's life, a new power, a new presence will reside within his lanky six-foot frame. For the romance and the beauty of Jed's marriage to remain, God (aka the real Prince Charming) must remain at the helm of Jed's life. He must be allowed to script his love story with Meri. Jed's job is to give God the control position at every turn throughout every day and allow the great heavenly Romantic to build him into a world-class husband. New habits must be made, while old habits must be broken. Jed must learn to give up his rights to everything he holds dear. He is no longer the master of his existence; he has been demoted to the head butler position. Whatever God, the new

Master of his estate, commands, he must learn to obey and put into action immediately. Jed's body will be officially taken over. He will be possessed by a superpower. And this power is love itself.

This is the process that each and every one of us must go through to emerge as a great spouse. It's not enough to promise our partner that we will be great in marriage. It's necessary to allow the God of the universe to daily build us into something tremendous.

Every single day is an opportunity to train and coordinate this new life and new power within. For instance, when your spouse says something hurtful or insensitive, your natural human response is to bite back with something equally hurtful. But in that moment, if instead you yield to the power of Christ within you, He equips you to respond to your spouse in *His* tender way, not in your own selfish way. He teaches you to *love your spouse as He loves you.*

Christ loves far differently than we love. He doesn't give or withhold His affection based on how we treat Him. He doesn't try to "balance the scales" or "even the score." He loves fully, completely, unconditionally, without thought to His own rights. He gives everything to us, though we are so undeserving of His selfless love. And when He overtakes our lives, that is how He trains us to love our spouses. Instead of giving to our spouses only as much as they deserve, we learn to give selflessly even if we don't receive the same in return. Instead of giving 50 percent to our marriages and expecting our spouses to give the other

50 percent, we learn to give 100 percent to our marriages, no matter what our spouses bring to the table. He trains us to lay down our rights and focus on giving rather than on getting. The more we yield to His divine life within us, the more we learn to treat our spouses with the supernatural love and self-lessness of Christ.

This has been the secret of the superheroic spouses down through the ages. They have learned to become ultimate lovers by first cultivating and maturing the life of the ultimate heavenly Lover within.

How hard is it to cultivate and mature this powerful new life? It is the hardest thing we will ever do outside of lying down on the operating table and submitting to the operating knife. Our bodies naturally want to reject this divine implant. We want to cling to our right to remain self-focused in our marriages. We want to hold on to our ability to live the way *we* want to, expecting our spouses to adjust around *our* agenda. In learning to share our lives with other humans, being Christlike can seem the most impossible task in the world—to be unconditionally selfless, servant-hearted, tender, forgiving, and understanding.

But God is more interested than even we are in bringing us through this process. It is not up to us to drum up the resolve to love our spouses as Christ loves us. It is His job to be the perfect Prince Charming. It is our job to get out of the way and allow Him to take center stage in our love stories.

Great spouses willingly submit to God's training, no matter

how difficult it is, no matter how rigorous and how painful the process, because they know the end result it brings. With every step of obedience, with every choice to treat your spouse as more important than yourself, with every decision to showcase God's love rather than your own selfish desires—the divine life of God grows more and more prominent and becomes more and more evident.

God knows what we can handle, and He is sure to never give us more difficulty than what we can bear at any moment. But don't confuse God with Santa Claus. He is by no means a softy with His children. He loves us too much to leave us as weaklings and sappy romantics who don't know how to truly protect our marriages. He trains His children to be like oak trees amid life's storms. Trust me, if you allow Him, He will transform you into an action hero fully capable of building one of the world's greatest marriages.

Most of us, like Jed, have attempted, in our own strength, to imitate Jesus Christ—to be tender and sensitive, caring and considerate at all times. After all, Christ is the most profound illustration of love this world has ever seen. To try to emulate Christ is a noble venture, but it isn't the way a mere human is supposed to go about becoming a superheroic spouse. It's not imitation but *impartation* that we need. Only when the life of God has been imparted can we possibly imitate *His* perfection in our marriages.

"It sounds just a little extreme, Eric," a young wife once said to me after I spoke about this concept to a roomful of couples. "Can't my marriage still work without me having to go through all of that?"

Extreme measures are needed to prepare you to be a great spouse because the battle over your marriage is extreme. Satan does not want your marriage to thrive through sickness and health, for richer or poorer, 'til death do you part. The enemy of your soul is also the enemy of your marriage. He is scared of God gaining control over your life. He realizes that he has absolutely no power over you as long as you are yielding to God and allowing His divinely implanted life—His supernatural power—to operate your existence. So Satan's goal in each and every moment of the day is to get you to turn back to your own powers, your own heart, your own mind to deal with the daily challenges of marriage. Just as kryptonite stripped Superman of all of his superpowers and drained him of all physical strength, so selfishness in taking control of your life from God will drain your strength and make you vulnerable to Satan's agenda in your life. Our arch nemesis has one very simple objective for each of our lives and marriages: to get us to fall into the trap of selfishness. He knows that if he can get us to protect and serve ourselves, our images, our wants, and our agendas, then our pockets will be stuffed full of kryptonite, and we will be emptied of all that is heroic and capable of true love. Our enemy wants us to reject the implanted life of Christ and retake the controls of our existence.

Satan is very aware that the kind of love capable of standing the test of time is selfless. Selfless love seeks your spouse's highest good—in the smallest tests, such as allowing your spouse to eat that last piece of cake or choose the movie on Saturday night, as well as in the most extreme tests of personal sacrifice known to man. Selfless love makes you willing not just to give up your right to the most comfortable chair, but to shed your *very blood* to showcase your extreme devotion to and affection for your spouse.

A great lover learns to live every moment as a selfless moment and therefore is always strong enough to fight for the beauty and excellence of married love.[1] We can't just swallow our spinach once and expect it to keep us strong for fifty years of marriage. As lovers in search of the purest, most perfect love, we must learn to yield to God's control over our lives—not just in the beginning of our marital ventures, but every moment of every day along the way.

I have told Leslie time and again that there isn't another man alive I would switch places with. I honestly believe I have not only the best wife on earth, but the sweetest, most magical marriage as well. I love my wife so much it hurts. The beauty of what we share together is indescribable. Day in and day out, we experience something that most people in this world have given up believing even exists—an amazing marriage.

But what we have has come with a price. We both have given

up countless personal ambitions and gratifying experiences so that we could make ourselves available to God and to each other. Our lives are owned and operated by the God of the universe, and He has taught us how to love, how to serve, how to sacrifice, how to give, and how to cherish our spouse's every little nuance.

The world may tell you that a perfect marriage is humanly impossible. And they are right. But God is in the business of pulling off the impossible in and through our lives if we allow Him to be the One in control. As far as I'm concerned, my marriage with Leslie is perfect. This is not to say it is absent of human error, but rather that it is a marriage in which our human weaknesses are constantly given over to God so that He can turn them into a picture of His almighty strength. And saying that our marriage is perfect isn't claiming that selfishness never rears its ugly head, but rather that selfishness is combated daily and viewed as the enemy it really is. It is perfect not because it is a completed masterpiece and all the rough spots have been smoothed, but because it is constantly moving in the direction of heavenly perfection. Our marriage is perfect because the ultimate Superhero has been invited into the center of our lives and our marriage to do as He sees fit.

Our marriage has cost us both everything. It has broken us, it has humbled us, it has proved to us how desperately in need of divine assistance we really are. But trust me when I say it has been worth ten thousand times over the price we've paid to get it.

It's my desire to have the world's greatest marriage. As a man, it is my desire to outdo every other husband as the noblest, most princely, most amazing husband ever. What about you? Are you going to let Leslie and I be the only ones experiencing all the marriage bliss? Or are you willing to do whatever it takes to find the same thing in your own marriage? Are you willing to fight for that taste of heaven on earth that God is ready to help you find?

In these first ninety days of your love as newlyweds, you must decide if you are willing to swallow your spinach and aim for the impossible or if you just want to remain everyday, mediocre lovers who share an everyday, mediocre love story. Remember, this is a book about marvelous marriages. It's a book about staying madly in love through all of life's ups and downs. It's a book about extraordinary sex. It's a book about discovering the ultimate purpose in marriage and winning its ultimate reward. But that reward will always seem to be dangling just out of reach in front of you down the raceway of life if you attempt to have these things in mere human strength. This is a book for superheroes—men and women made into extraordinary spouses by the extraordinary life of God within.

Not even a single instant of life is wasted that is spent in the pursuit of learning to love as Christ loves.

So let the games begin! And may God decide when it is all said and done which one of us has won first prize. Here's to a lifetime of the most exquisite pleasure and a million rides into the sunset!

Putting It into Action

- Leslie -

Step #1: Adopt a Marriage Mission Statement

Don't ever become apathetic in your quest for a Christ-centered marriage.

It takes focus and commitment to fight daily for your marriage relationship. It means submitting afresh to God's desires each and every morning. It means giving up your own rights each moment of the day. It means not allowing Satan to creep in and undermine the superheroic power of Christ within by convincing you to cling to your own selfish agenda. It's important to have a clear vision of what you are fighting for so you don't ever become apathetic in your quest for a Christ-centered marriage that stands the test of time.

Eric and I have found that having a marriage mission statement helps remind us of God's vision for our marriage. It keeps us focused on what we are fighting to protect on a daily basis. Our marriage mission statement is this:

To have a marriage relationship that is a reflection of the love relationship we share with our true Bridegroom, Jesus Christ. To be faithful to each other in every way—heart, mind, soul, and body—for as long as we both shall live. To serve and love each other selflessly, unconditionally, the way Christ loves us. To seek each other's highest good and lay down our lives for each other, as Christ laid down His life for us. To experience marriage the way God intended it to be—as a little taste of heaven on earth.

Individually, take some time to think and pray about God's purpose for your marriage. Write down the words or sentences that best describe the goals and desires God has given you for your new marriage relationship. Share them with your spouse. Based on what each of you has written and discussed, decide together what your marriage mission statement will be. Then craft your mission statement in a few sentences or paragraphs that express God's purpose for your marriage.

As a couple, take some time to pray specifically for God to supernaturally enable you to live out the words you have written in your mission statement. In your own human strength, you won't be able to fulfill God's expectations for your marriage. Unless He is at the center of your love, your marriage mission statement will be only some hollow words on a piece of paper. But if the Author of romance is your foundation, you will be amazed at what can happen in and through your marriage relationship. He alone can make the words you have written in your mission statement into so much more than wishful thinking—He can weave those words into the very fabric of your daily life.

It's a good idea to place your marriage mission statement where you can see it often—you may even want to type it up, laminate it, and put a copy in your wallet. Your marriage mission statement reminds you to never settle for mediocrity, to always keep pursuing more and more of the beauty God has awaiting you. It helps spur you on to greatness, like that Olympic athlete with his eye on the gold medal. And anytime you are having conflict or discouragement in your marriage relationship, take out your marriage mission statement and read it—together if possible. As hard as this may be to do in the heat of emotion, it will remind you why God brought you together and help you both refocus on what is truly important. It will help keep you headed toward the same destination, even in the midst of life's ups and downs.

Step #2: Exchange Your Expectations

Surrender is not a onetime act; is a daily, moment-by-moment decision.

Surrendering your life to the God of the universe is a very personal decision. No one else can make it for you. As a couple, set aside some time when both of you can be alone and individually evaluate where God is in your lives and hearts. If possible, go to a quiet place where you won't be interrupted. You may want to have a pen and some paper ready. If you have already given God the pen of your life, renew your commitment to let Him script your life and love story in His own perfect time and way. And if you have never invited the King of all kings to be the Ruler over every part of your life, now is the time to relinquish control. As long as *you* hold the pen of your life, you won't be able to script anything more than a mediocre marriage at best. It's only when God has complete access to your inner life that He can transform you into a heroic spouse.

Here are some things to consider during your time of soul-searching and waiting on God. As stated earlier, surrender is not a onetime act; it is a daily, moment-by-moment decision. It's not enough just to let Him write your story *before* marriage—He wants to continue to script your love story even *after* you take your vows. Allow God to shine His light into your soul. Ask Him to show you anything you are clinging to, anything you are unwilling to let Him have access to. As stated earlier, success comes when you exchange your own human hopes and dreams for God's heavenly ones. When it comes to marriage, many of us have self-built expectations and ideals that must be replaced with *God's* plans and desires for lifelong romance.

For example, the first few months that Eric and I were married turned out to be far different from anything I ever would have expected. We moved from a warm climate to subzero temperatures in a small Michigan town that, to me, was in the middle of nowhere. We lived in a bed-and-breakfast that had closed down for the winter. In the summer it was a gorgeous place, with a shimmering lake and beautiful trees. But when we lived there, the lake was frozen, the trees were barren, and the skies were gloomy. The house seemed big and creepy (like the setting for a horror movie), especially when Eric left for work each morning in our one car, and I was stuck there all day by myself. And things only seemed to get worse as the weeks went by.

I woke up one morning to find my legs covered in bug bites. The house turned out to be infested with fleas. It was disgusting—we could actually see them jumping out of the carpet. A few days later, I heard strange noises coming from the fireplace. A family of raccoons had moved in for the winter, haunting me with their scratching and clawing all day long, filling my mind with images of rabid animals breaking down the fireplace door and chasing me around the house. We couldn't seem to get rid of the raccoons or the fleas, no matter what we tried. We set off "flea bombs" in our house, which only seemed to make the fleas multiply. I, on the other hand, developed an allergic reaction to the chemicals and ended up with a severe bronchial infection that kept me in bed for a month. And then our pipes burst and flooded our kitchen, destroying our washing machine in the process. So two months into our "happily-ever-after marriage," I was sick in bed with a horrible cough, covered with flea bites, listening to raccoons fight in the fireplace, and surrounded by piles of dirty clothes. This was a far cry from the cute little home with the white picket fence that I'd always imagined!

God challenged me to give Him the pen of my life afresh; to lay down *my* agenda, *my* expectations, and *my* plans for what our married life was supposed to be; to allow Him to take us through whatever trials and challenges He saw fit; to let Him continue to script our love story in His own perfect way. I realized that I'd subconsciously been thinking of marriage as the time when "everything would finally be perfect" in my life, when I would be completely satisfied and fulfilled simply because I was finally married. But I was looking for satisfaction in human things—in having a comfortable home, a white picket fence, and a husband who knew how to meet all of my needs.

After spending time doing some serious soul-searching, I was reminded that my number one source of fulfillment and satisfaction must be Christ alone. My external circumstances might never be perfect. My marriage to Eric, though wonderful, could never fulfill the deepest needs of my heart. But my relationship with the God of the universe *could* satisfy and fulfill me completely, if I would simply surrender my entire life to Him.

In eleven years of marriage to Eric, my expectations have been shaken many times. We've experienced everything from financial struggles to health struggles to extremely difficult ministry challenges and disappointments. But through it all, our marriage has thrived. God has held the pen and scripted our story, and though each chapter turns out differently than we would have imagined, we have found time and again that the Author of romance always knows what He is doing. God's being in control, scripting our story, is what has given us the deepest, truest form of fulfillment that marriage can offer. And whenever we begin to take the pen back and try to manipulate things to turn out *our* way, He gently reminds us that true satisfaction is found only when He is in control.

Think about your own expectations for married life. Are you hoping for the cute home with the white picket fence, financial security, sterling health, three perfect children, and a great retirement plan? Are you expecting your spouse to be the person of your dreams twenty-four hours a day? If so, you likely are in for some disappointment. Sure, God might allow you to have seasons of health and financial security. And yes, there may be times when your spouse completely fulfills the romantic dreams of your heart. But if you are looking to your circumstances to bring you satisfaction, and if you are turning to your spouse to meet all of your deepest needs, you will be disappointed somewhere along the line. Let Christ have His way, even if it means giving up everything you ever hoped for in life. Let Christ be your source of true fulfillment, even when your spouse lets you down. Your life may never look exactly the way you pictured it, but you will find satisfaction and security that can't be shaken by the circumstances or disappointments of life.

Allow yourself to be brought under God's surgical knife. He must remove anything that stands in the way of complete surrender to Him. Allow Him to take your human dreams, hopes, and expectations and replace them with *His* agenda for your life and your marriage—whatever that may be. Only when you allow God to surgically alter you, own you, and operate you can you truly be prepared to experience "happily ever after" even in the midst of fleas, raccoons, and whatever challenges life throws your way.

Step #3: Replace Selfish Habits

Marriage is a constant decision to either yield to Christ or yield to your selfish wants.

Training to be a superheroic spouse starts with learning to yield to Christ each moment of the day. After inviting Christ to take over our inner lives, most of us continue to go our own merry ways, acting as we've always acted and doing the things we've always done. To learn to love our spouses as Christ loves, we must learn to get out of the way and let Christ live His life through us. That means our old habits have to die. We must retrain our responses. We must choose a new "default printer" for our internal computers.

During the daily challenges of life, most of us have developed selfish habits. This is especially true in marriage. Marriage is a constant decision to either yield to Christ or yield to your selfish wants. You want the comfortable chair, you want to choose how to spend your time on Saturday afternoon, you want to decide where to keep your mountain bike (what's wrong with the living room floor?), and you want your spouse to constantly meet your needs and serve your desires.

Now, Christ wants to reprogram you to be concerned with what *He* wants, not what you want. Christ is far less concerned with helping you get "what you need out of this marriage" than He is with teaching you to yield to Him, to sacrifice your own personal agenda, and to lay down your life in service for your spouse, even if he or she is undeserving.

As a couple, plan a time when both of you can be alone and individually evaluate the habits of your life together thus far. Have pen and paper ready, and prayerfully ask God to reveal to you any selfish habits you may have already adopted. Do you fight for the comfortable chair, control of the remote, the last piece of cake? Guys, do you ignore your wife's pleas to pick up your dirty clothes, spend more time with her on the weekends, or turn off the computer at night simply because you are holding on to your "right" to do things your way? Girls, do you manipulate your husband into serving your own agenda? Do you give him the silent treatment when he says something insensitive to you? Do you regularly ignore his desire for sex just because you "aren't in the mood"?

Allow God to show you any area in which you have been acting selfishly in your new life with your spouse. And then ask Him to show you how *Christ* would have you respond in those areas. For each selfish habit you write down, write the Christlike response next to it. Guys, if you are used to spending Saturday afternoons watching sports on TV because it is your "right," the new Christlike response might be turning off the television this Saturday and asking your wife how you can be sensitive to *her* desires during the weekend. Girls, if you are used to "pouting" whenever your husband says or does something that bothers you, the new Christlike response might be graciously addressing the issue with your husband in a loving and respectful way.

Even if you haven't been married long enough to form obvious selfish habits, you still may have brought selfish *attitudes* into your marriage. Do you inwardly expect your spouse to bend around your agenda, your plans, and your wants? Do you subconsciously think of your house, your possessions, and your time as your own, to do with as you please? If so, allow Christ to replace these selfish attitudes with *His* selfless, servant-hearted ones.

Remember, Christ is not concerned with "balancing the scales" or "evening the score." He hasn't called you to give 50 percent to your marriage and expect your spouse to give the other 50. He asks you to give 100 percent to your marriage, even if your spouse is not giving 100 percent in return. So don't focus on your spouse's selfish habits. Just focus on dealing with your own.

Make it your focus to begin putting these new, Christlike habits into practice, starting right now. Be aware that it will take time for heavenly habits to replace the old selfish ones. As you are learning to yield to Christ's desires instead of your own, it may seem awkward and uncomfortable. The selfish part of you may rebel and fight for control. But the more you lay down your own agenda and yield to Christ's desires, the more natural and habitual these new responses will become. Imagine a piece of black construction paper enfolded around a bright lightbulb. If a small hole is poked in the paper, a beam of light makes its way through the stark black texture. And the larger that hole becomes, the greater the amount of light that cascades through the darkness. The more you (the black construction paper) learn to get out of the way, the more Christ's light will shine through your life. The less your spouse sees of you, the more your spouse will see of Him.

In a Nutshell

Mere human romanticism won't cut it when it comes to achieving greatness in marriage. Roses and rhymes are wonderful, but in and of themselves, they won't make a marriage something to behold. In fact, a perfect marriage is possible only when we, as human spouses, submit to God's operating table and go under His operating knife. Superhero spouses are born when the superheroic life of God is surgically implanted within and the ultimate Prince Charming is allowed to love in and through us.

When God surgically implants Himself into a human body, His superhero development has only just begun. He doesn't make great lovers overnight—He crafts them over time. He trains them like athletes; He builds them like action heroes. And in the end, His goal is to make them look, act, and love just like Him.

Cultivating and maturing this God-life within is the ancient secret of every truly masterful husband or wife throughout history. When Christ is allowed to reside within and make our bodies His princely domain, He trains us to love as He loves, serve as He serves, and forgive as He forgives. As husband and wife, our job isn't to script for ourselves a great love story. It is simply to give Him the pen and allow Him to direct the amazing drama.

Chapter Two

HOW TO STAY MADLY IN LOVE THROUGH LIFE'S UPS AND DOWNS

To a great lover, the difficulties of marriage are the cherished moments in which a love can be proved authentic.

- Eric -

In the movies, great lovers are the sexy, hot hard-bodies that know how to find their way into the bedroom by the second date. We all have grown up in a culture that emphasizes externals and equates body weight, body shape, lip contour, cheekbone height, and length of lashes with great love. Hollywood can paint powerful love stories on the silver screen, but in real life the actors and actresses in those movies prove daily that the love theories espoused by the film industry simply don't work. Sexy men and women might sell movies, magazines, and deodorant, but a sexy body doesn't in and of itself make a marriage work, make a marriage last, or make a marriage beautiful.

Great lovers in real life are not focused on getting their clothes off and slipping under the covers for a little five-minute magic. Great lovers in real life don't have to speak with a sultry voice, starve themselves to maintain their weight, and deliver slick pickup lines to win their romantic objectives. Rather, great real-world lovers are great simply because they know how to cherish and adore their spouses. They are great because they know how to serve even when the serving isn't easy or even romantic. They know how to forgive and be forgivable even when it is painful to their pride. Great lovers in real life aren't suave sex gurus, they are masters of knowing how to make their spouses feel like the most important, most loved persons on earth.

This isn't to say there is no hope for you if you are one of *People* magazine's fifty most beautiful people in the world. There is certainly nothing wrong with being externally beautiful, and I'm sure your spouse would agree. But what makes a marriage work isn't the way a lover looks, but the way a lover chooses to live. Physical beauty does have a value in a marriage. But it's a value that, in our modern culture, has been blown out of proportion from what God intended it to be. Great marriages are the result of spouses who groom themselves internally and not just externally. They don't just wear deodorant and gargle with mouthwash; they maintain their spiritual and emotional hygiene as well. Great lovers may not, on the outside, look like Brad Pitt or Angelina Jolie, but on the *inside*, they are drop-dead gorgeous.

If you want to stay madly in love with your spouse through all of life's ups and downs, you're going to need more than looks. You need to become a legendary beauty on the inside.

Bulging muscles on the outside may serve you well in opening a jar of pickles, but sculpted muscles on the *inside* are what enable you to open up the armory of heaven and fight valiantly for marriage intimacy.

Building Your Inner Physique

It's always bothered Leslie and me to see married couples, after as few as five months of marriage, begin to completely abandon their efforts to look good for each other. Leslie and I made commitments to one another when we were first married to always seek to look our best physically for each other. We don't try to stay up with the culture's standard for buffness or beauty, but we do our best to stay physically in shape as a gift to each other. I often say no to the Pop-Tart for breakfast and the slice of pecan pie à la mode for dessert, because Leslie is always on my mind. I want to be a strong man for her, not one who is wedged into his recliner and unable to prove a courageous protector. As a result, I use rice milk, eat soy ice cream, spread coconut oil on my toast, and mix a weird green powder every morning mixed into a glass of orange juice. I eat this odd assortment of foods not because they taste better to me than whole milk, ice cream, and butter, but because I will do anything to show my wife how seriously I take being her man.

If you have ever physically trained your body, you know you can't measure the value of getting in shape by "how fun" the process is. The value of getting in shape, whereas it doesn't have to be a miserable process, must be measured by the end results. None of us would dream of getting up at 4:45 in the morning to go jump into a frigid cold lake for a triathlon training session if it were merely for the free PowerBar and the opportunity to wear that attractive Speedo.

In other words, most of us already realize that the pains of getting in shape are worth the end result of actually *being* in shape. In fact, it's quite extraordinary that when you work through the first months of "getting in shape," training actually becomes fun. No, it doesn't get easier, but it's strangely energizing when you see your body responding, growing, and strengthening.

Leslie appreciates the fact that I work hard to keep my external physique healthy and strong, but it would mean nothing to her if I weren't first and foremost caring for my *inner* physique. Training an inner physique is an odd concept to many, but in many ways it is no different than building a bicep or training a cardiovascular system. It is hard work and demands extreme discipline, avid consistency, and stalwart perseverance.

Many of us know what it is like to make our New Year's resolutions, head to the health club for two weeks straight, and then never go again. It's sad, but most health clubs bring in more than half their revenue from our hollow "resolutions" to get in shape. But don't let training your inner physique become just another New Year's resolution. If you don't get into physical shape, your health will be affected; but if you don't train your inner physique, your marriage, your family, your friendships, and most important, your relationship with God will be affected.

A well-groomed and finely crafted inner physique is the single most beautiful thing on planet Earth. The world may not have eyes to see its grandeur, but anyone with the ability to see what heaven sees will be drawn like a moth to the flame of its sublime magnificence. A polished inner physique has a greater form of muscle than that of a finely carved bicep. It's the kind of strength that can lead men to battle, die a martyr's death, shrug off public opinion, admit wrong and appear a fool, fight for the poor and the outcast, love the unlovable, and forsake self to seek God's agenda no matter the cost to life and limb. This is not only the kind of strength that makes a marriage amazing, but the kind of strength that changes the world.

Granted, to speak of an internal muscle is a bit bizarre, mainly because most of us have never known that we can build unseen muscles. Courage, faith, love, compassion, loyalty—these are just a few of the individual sinews that lie within our hearts, awaiting our resolve to build them into something grand.

Tensile Strength

Let's give this interior muscle a name. Leslie and I call it tensile strength. Tensile strength is a different form of strength than muscular strength. It's made up not of physical muscular tissue and sinew, but of spiritual substance. It's not the type of muscle that grows bigger with use; it's the type of muscle that becomes more toned, capable, and coordinated with use.

The strength of rope is measured by the term *tensile strength*. Great weights are tied to the rope and then dropped to test the resiliency of the rope under stress. The greater the ability of the rope to endure weight and combative force, the stronger the tensile rating.

Our hearts are measured for life and marriage the very same way. If we have never focused on building our tensile strength, then even the smallest weights and stresses will cause us to snap. But if we are willing to build our tensile strength and train like an Olympian, our souls will be able to endure weights even as gargantuan as imprisonment and torture. The heroic Christians throughout history who gave up their lives in such astounding ways were the ones who trained their inner physiques to handle the greatest pressures and stresses life could throw their way.

The ups and downs of married love are too much for the man and woman with a weak tensile rating. Paul the apostle said that "those who marry will face many troubles" (1 Corinthians 7:28 NIV). He wasn't exaggerating. Marriage brings out a whole host of challenges that a single person can't even comprehend. And the married couple who prove cowardly and weak in the pressure cooker of covenant love will certainly never find that taste of heaven on earth. To have a successful marriage, you need to build up the strength of your inner life. The many pleasures of married love are discovered in direct proportion to the quality of the two spouses' inner physiques. So let's discuss how tensile strength is built.

The training ground for tensile strength isn't a health club across town, but rather your own home. The opportunities to train can't be scheduled to fit around your meals, work time, and leisure activities—they are constant, presenting themselves with unabated zeal every minute of every day. To train in tensile strength, you have to keep your eyes wide open for each opportunity and then aggressively grab it and take advantage of it. You can't expect tensile strength to grow on its own just because you desire to have it; you have to be willing to do whatever it takes to build it stronger every day.

One of my biggest opportunities for building tensile strength was while Leslie was pregnant with our son, Hudson. I have always been extremely protective of my sleep. With great discipline I would go to bed at 9:30 in the evening and be up to meet the day at half past five. "I need eight hours of rest!" I would proclaim. Enter a pregnant woman having to get up fifty-seven times a night to use the bathroom (not much of an exaggeration!). She would feel sick to her stomach, roll over and place her hand on my chest, and sweetly say, "Beef, I need a glass of water," or twenty minutes later, "Beef, is there any way you could get me a bowl of cereal?" I'm sure you can anticipate the potential friction. But I had begun a program, months earlier, to train my interior physique. I was ready for this one. I decided that every time an opportunity presented itself to build my tensile, I would embrace it with eagerness, a spring in my step, and a giant smile plastered across my face.

So there I was, in the depths of the sweetest sleep, and I would feel, for what seemed like the fifty-seventh time that night, Leslie's hand upon my chest. "Tensile strength!" I would whisper to myself, then hop out of bed with a sleepy smile. The kitchen just happens to feel a good three miles away in the middle of the night. I would receive orders from my princess and venture out into the hallway in my boxer shorts. I would wobble down the stairs and make sure I had a cheerful spring in my step. I didn't use this time just to build tensile, but I also decided to pray for our little boy squirming in Leslie's womb. As I fumbled through the pantry trying to find the specific kind of cereal that Leslie "had to have," I could feel the growth taking place within me. It wasn't the fact that I prepared her a bowl of cereal in the middle of the night that was building me; it was the eagerness, the willingness, and the love with which I poured that bowlful of cereal that were growing me.

These kinds of opportunities are everywhere every day. The moments you are challenged to be either selfish or selfless with a situation, the moments you are greeted with an opportunity to take an easier, less-noble road or a harder, more Christlike road—these are tensile-strength opportunities. These are the moments that can either make you great or make you a schmuck. But then remember, it's not just doing the right thing, but doing it with the right attitude. Believe it or not, when you learn to jump out of bed in your boxer shorts and say, "How can I serve you?" it actually becomes fun.

When Hudson was first born, I thought all my training in tensile strength was going to make parenting a breeze. (Cough!) Instead, I realized that the tensile-strength opportunities had only just begun in my life. Still to this day, Leslie and I are both convinced that neither of us slept for the first four months of his life. Getting three bowls of cereal and four glasses of water in the night for Leslie during her pregnancy now seemed like a far-away dreamland of ease.

Hudson needed food every three hours, even in the middle of the night. He had severe intestinal problems and acid reflux and was therefore often in excruciating pain. He would cry, and Leslie and I would hop out of bed and mumble to each other, "Tensile strength!" Every parent who has faced an extreme infancy with their baby knows what I mean when I say I wouldn't choose to go through that again. However, even though it was possibly the hardest thing Leslie and I have ever endured, it was an amazing opportunity for tensile growth. Most people miss the juiciest opportunities for tensile-strength development because they are too busy mumbling and complaining, wishing their circumstances would change. Whenever we allow selfish perspective to gain a voice in our inner worlds, our tensile muscles begin to grow flabby and we become vulnerable to a marriage snap.

There are a thousand opportunities in each day to hone your inner physique. But if you are not aggressively seeking tensile growth, you will miss every last one of them. Learn to eagerly embrace every trial that you encounter, learn to smile, and don't forget to make sure you have that all-important kick in your step. It will take a bit of time, but pretty soon what was a focused effort on your part will become a habit. And when seizing opportunities for tensile growth becomes a habit in your life, the stage is set for an amazing marriage.

Becoming a Marriage Hero

Heroes aren't made in the shade, but in the heat of life's battles. They relish the fight and view the challenges as opportunities to prove their moral worth. Great lovers are made the very same way. To great lovers, the difficulties of marriage are the cherished moments that their love can finally be defined and proved authentic.

Unfortunately, most of us miss out on these golden opportunities. Take Carl, a new groom who is disappointed with marriage. "I thought marriage was going to be a blast," he told me. "Instead, it's just one fight after the next. Honestly, I don't see why anyone does this!"

Today, young husbands and wives often aren't prepared for the fiery pressures of marriage intimacy. They ignorantly expected sex all day and all night long, and instead they found that their hearts and souls came under siege to a thousand moral choices set to prove them romantic frauds. As a result of this unexpected onslaught, most slink into an emotional fortress and close their eyes, hoping it will all go away. They cut off emotionally from their spouses and slip into a catatonic self-preservation mode.

But as difficult as marriage can be to the unsuspecting and unprepared spouse, so in contrast, the wise spouse, prepared to fight for what's really important, views every challenge of wedded life as something to cherish and embrace. The wise lover sees marriage as the training ground for tensile strength.

Tensile strength is the growl of the godly soul—the power to act rightly in a wrong world. It's the measure of one's ability to handle the stress and pressures of life. Tensile strength is the stuff of champions. It's the thing that causes a boxer to get up from his stool in round 15 and keep fighting; it's the thing that causes a hero to lunge in front of a speeding car to rescue the little boy even at the peril of his own life. Tensile strength is the intangible item that separates those willing to die for Christ and those who cower when their loyalties are called into question. Tensile strength is what sets apart those who are inspired by life's challenges and those who are buried beneath them.

Masculine Tensile Strength

In some ways, tensile strength in men and women is different. For us men it produces masculine nobility, while in women it creates feminine dignity. This is partly due to the fact that we as men are called of God to apply our strengths in different ways than women are. For instance, men are called to be initiators and protectors. God designed men to be the stronger sex both physically and emotionally, and thus, He expects us to take the hits, to stand in front of the oncoming bullets and become a shield for the ones we love.

In a premarriage season of love, a man is responsible for being the vulnerable one in initiating the progression of a romance. We must be the ones willing to take the rejection. We are also responsible for the protection of the physical nature of the relationship as it progresses toward marriage. We are the knights in shining armor who must relinquish our physical desires to assure that our girls are protected and preserved for God's highest and best and that their purity is held sacred.

In marriage, a man's tensile strength is taxed in even more challenging ways than in the premarriage season of love. In marriage, he is still an initiator and a protector, but now he has an even greater weight of responsibility. As the husband, he is now the protector of the *unity* of the marriage. If there is ever an argument or a lover's spat, the responsibility falls on his shoulders to initiate forgiveness and reconciliation. And the man is responsible for acting quickly. A man weak in tensile strength will want to wait until the awkwardness of

Present coupon at time of purchase. Limit one coupon per person, per visit. Valid through December 31, 2007. Offer valid on in-store purchases only. Not valid with other coupons or disco Photocopies or falsified coupons will not be accepted.

Cashier Instructions: Scan all merchandise. At the enter SKU Prompt, press F9 Discounts. Select Ap To: 'I' ITEM. Select item level %. Enter the discount amount 100. Press enter at the "warning" prom At the Select A Reason Prompt, Type in the "0000 – MCC Coffee" Reason Code.

asking forgiveness has lessened. But great masculine nobility is quick to recognize error and quick to make it right, even at the expense of his pride.

Without toned tensile in his soul, a husband can't properly love his wife. Many a husband thinks it is unfair that he must ask forgiveness for his small role in a marital conflict even when his wife seems to have made a far greater contribution to the fracas.

Mike, a young husband of two months, recently complained, "I don't see why I should have to constantly say, 'I'm sorry,' when she never apologizes to me for anything!" Too many men are after equity in marriage. "I did this for you; now you owe me something." That attitude is not noble and reveals a lack of tensile strength. A great husband is willing to allow for inequity. He is willing to take full responsibility for every single argument, if necessary, to maintain the unity and peace in his home. Just as Christ went to the cross and suffered pain that rightly belonged to His bride, so a great husband must be willing to suffer a cross daily in order to protect and serve the *unity* of his love.

Again, this masculine nobility is not inherent in a man; it must be built. Tensile strength is not developed overnight, but over a lifetime. Husbands, don't despair if you find a bit more knucklehead than noble knight in your behavior when you are first married. If you haven't been a heroic protector in your relationship with your wife (either before your marriage or after), start by asking her forgiveness. Declare your commitment to be the protector of your marriage and the initiator of reconciliation when conflict arises. Then begin looking for every tensile opportunity that comes along. As you willingly embrace each of these opportunities, your wife will soon begin to see the heavenly hunk of her dreams emerge.

- Leslie -

Feminine Tensile Strength

As a woman, God has called you to be a rock for your husband—a strong, dependable force he can count on through any circumstance. When the challenges of life hit, either you can become an emotionally fragile mess, concerned with protecting your own comfort and security, or you can be a pillar of tensile strength, the one who will inspire and equip your husband to be everything Christ has called him to be.

When I think of feminine tensile strength, I often think of Sabina Wurmbrandt, a pastor's wife in Communist Romania in the 1940s. Sabina was a small woman with huge tensile strength. She and her husband, Richard, were attending a convention of Romanian pastors during the time of the Communist takeover. Pastor after pastor was publicly committing loyalty to the Communist government rather than Christ. Sabina knew these men were speaking heresy in order to save their own lives, but she could not bear to hear the name of Christ blasphemed. She turned to her husband. "Will you not wash this shame from the face of Christ, Richard?" Her husband looked around at the assembled delegates and government officials. He knew what opening his mouth would cost—his freedom, and perhaps even his very life. "If I go up and speak," he told Sabina, "they will kill me!" Sabina looked him straight in the eyes and replied that she would rather have a dead man for a husband than a coward.[1]

Flooded with new resolve, Richard Wurmbrandt stood, walked slowly to the platform, took the microphone, and spoke words of truth—words that cost him fourteen years of imprisonment and torture, words that cost Sabina years of persecution as well. Out of the hundreds of Christian ministers there that day, Richard was the only one who was willing to risk everything in order to preserve the name of Christ. What did Richard have that the other men did not? A wife with great tensile strength. A woman who put her commitment to Christ far above her selfish human desires. A woman who boldly equipped her husband to be everything that God wanted him to be—even at the expense of her own comfort, security, and happiness.

Don't expect your husband to always be the strong one in your marriage while you allow yourself to be an emotional roller coaster. Sure, your husband will be a pillar of strength for you during times of sadness or confusion. But it isn't just a one-way street. Your husband needs the same from you. Marriage is about leaning on each other—strengthening each other in times of weakness. Allow Christ to shape you into a woman like Sabina Wurmbrandt, to help you become that unmoving rock your husband can draw courage and inspiration from during every storm. When your husband is weak, be his pillar of strength. When your husband is worried, help him see from a heavenly perspective. And when your husband needs a loving kick in the behind, be willing to administer it!

It is important to note that there is a huge difference between Christ-built tensile strength and human manipulation (aka nagging). It is tempting to try to manipulate and control your husband to get him to be a stronger man. A young wife named Brandi told me, "I am so tired of him being a wimp. He doesn't have any vision. He needs to be more of a leader in our marriage. And the more I tell him this, the less he listens to me." Nagging your husband will only tear down his masculinity and make him even less of a confident leader. As women, we must be sure that we are yielding to Christ's agenda rather than our own selfish ones. We must not use our own manipulative devices to control our husbands. Instead, we must allow *Christ* to shape us into women of great tensile strength—women who are led not by emotion, but by truth. A woman with great tensile strength is one who encourages, motivates, and strengthens her husband through her unwavering trust in Christ.

If you are unsure how to begin your development of feminine tensile strength, start with the next trial that comes your way. No matter how big or small the challenge may be, don't immediately turn inward, worried about protecting your own interests. Instead, turn to Christ. Fall on your knees and submit the entire situation to Him. Allow Him to flood you with His perspective—read the Psalms and be reminded that He is in loving control. Allow Him to give you His perspective about the trial you are facing. He is not wringing His hands in worry. He is utterly confident. He knows the ending of the story, and He has your highest good in mind. So don't cave in to anxiety and fear. Don't give in to the stress of this world. Be like Sarah, Abraham's wife, who, though her circumstances seemed impossible, put her entire trust in the sovereignty of God. The Bible says that we are her daughters if we "do what is right without being frightened by any fear" (1 Peter 3:6 NASB).

Each time you stand strong rather than crumbling under the weights of the world, you will build tensile strength, one challenge at a time. Soon, you will begin to handle bigger and bigger stresses with Christ-built strength rather than caving in to human anxiety and fear. And if the moment comes when you need to pull a Sabina Wurmbrandt and help your husband be all that Christ wants him to be, you will have the courage to fulfill your high calling.

Tensile strength is the stuff of champions, the stuff of super-heroic spouses. Don't settle for a rubber spine and a flabby heart when a backbone of steel and a courageous soul are waiting to be had. Learn to embrace the everyday challenges of life. Let the challenges be your tutors; let the difficulties be your trainers. For if you do, you will never lack tensile strength in your time of need.

Here's to going the distance with style and grace!

Putting It into Action

Step #1: Develop the Right Conflict Habits (Leslie)

If you develop the right conflict habits early in your marriage, you can avoid the walls of bitterness that build up over the years between most husbands and wives.

Conflict, arguments, and disagreements are excellent tensile-strength "growth opportunities" in your marriage. As we discussed earlier, the perfect marriage is not one without conflict, but one in which conflict serves to hone your tensile strength and deepen your love for each other. If conflict is not handled in a Christlike way, it will slowly erode your foundation and weaken your marriage. But it takes great tensile strength to utilize conflict as a marriage-building tool rather than taking the easy way out and letting conflict drive wedges between you and your spouse. If you develop the right habits for dealing with conflict early in your marriage, you can avoid the walls of bitterness that build up over the years between most husbands and wives. Every argument can actually serve to enhance your commitment to each other, if you approach it God's way. In your first ninety days of marriage, take some time to sit down as a couple and develop a plan for handling conflict in a Christlike way by choosing to put the following principles into practice:

Conflict Habit #1: Be Quick to Admit You Are Wrong.
Someone once said that your humility can be measured by
how quickly you admit you are wrong. Though it is uncomfortable and damaging to your pride, if you ask forgiveness
from your spouse *the moment* you realize you have wronged
him or her, you won't waste hours having huge fights over
small issues. You will show your spouse that you value your
marriage relationship even more than your pride, and you
will develop great tensile strength as a result. The next time
you realize that you have hurt your spouse, done something
insensitive, or been selfish in your attitude, immediately ask
his or her forgiveness. It may be painful at first, but the more
you put it into practice, the more it will become a Christlike
habit in your life. You will find that your spouse's love and
respect for you only grow when you are willing to humble
yourself by quickly admitting your faults.

Conflict Habit #2: Don't Keep Score. Even if your spouse's
part in a conflict seems much more substantial than yours, deal
with *your* part, and let your spouse deal with his or her own.
Husbands, it isn't your job to make sure your wife is respecting
you or submitting to your leadership. That is between her and
God. Your only job is to love her as Christ loves you and to be
worthy of her respect no matter how she acts in return. Wives,
the same is true for you. Don't withhold affection, kindness,
and respect from your husband according to how Christlike he
is (or isn't) toward you. Love and respect him even when he

doesn't deserve it. Let God be the One to show him his areas of weakness. If you yield to Him, Christ will offer you the grace and strength you need to keep your own slate clean regardless of how messy the other person's slate may be.

Conflict Habit #3: Move Past Your Past. If you dishonored your spouse prior to marriage by giving your heart, mind, and/or body to another person, take time to sit down with your spouse and ask forgiveness for giving away something that was meant for only the two of you. And if your spouse dishonored *you* in the past, offer complete forgiveness. And then move on. In this new marriage, Christ has offered you a new beginning, a fresh start. Don't allow past mistakes to cloud your marriage relationship. When Christ forgives us, He removes our sins as far away from us as the east is from the west. That is how He wants us to forgive each other. If you let Him, Christ will give you "heavenly eyes" to see your spouse as He does—clean and whole, not marred by past failures. So adopt Christ's perspective, and don't hold your spouse's past mistakes over him or her. Don't try to make your spouse feel guilty. Once the past has been dealt with, don't dig it up again. Decide now that you will not let past mistakes become a part of your new life together.

Additionally, when conflict in your marriage comes, deal with it and then move on. Make up your mind that you will not continually dredge up past hurts, reminding your spouse of every time he or she ever let you down. Don't use your spouse's past mistakes as weapons against him or her during times of conflict. Marriages crumble when couples can't let go of past wrongs. Agree together that you won't use phrases such as "you always" or "you never" when discussing marriage issues. Let each conflict stand alone rather than blurring all your spouse's mistakes together into one big marital mishap. Be gracious and understanding toward your spouse. Give your spouse room to change and to grow. Protect your marriage by letting past hurts *stay* in the past and not become part of your future.

Conflict Habit #4: Don't Go to Bed Angry. The Bible says, "Do not let the sun go down on your anger" (Ephesians 4:26 NASB). This is an important principle for conflict in marriage. When conflict is not dealt with, it takes root in the soil of your marriage, growing into weeds of bitterness and pain that can choke the life out of your love story. Decide early in your marriage that you will not go to bed when there is unresolved conflict between you. Don't let small frustrations or hurts grow into bigger ones. Even if you must stay up late talking, cancel your dinner plans, or turn off the movie you wanted to watch, protecting the unity in your relationship is well worth the sacrifice.

Even after eleven years of marriage, Eric and I don't carry around bitterness and resentment toward each other for past hurts. This isn't because we never hurt each other—far from it. Rather, our marriage slate is kept clean because we deal with issues as soon as they arise. It's a conflict habit we developed when we were first married, and it has made an incredible difference in our relationship. Never once have we gone to bed angry with each other—even if it meant we had to stay up all night talking it out and making things right. We kill the seeds of bitterness before they have a chance to grow. We wake up each morning knowing that things are right between us.

Note: If you encounter a conflict situation in your marriage that you can't seem to work through together, then consider working with a pastor or biblical counselor. Often a godly perspective from the outside can help bring clarity to a cloudy issue. Do what you must to keep minor conflict from growing into major resentment that can undermine your entire relationship.

Conflict Habit #5: Honor Your Marriage Covenant. When you spoke your wedding vows, you pledged to love and cherish your spouse for the rest of your life. A marriage is not a casual contract, easily nullified when things get difficult. A marriage is a sacred covenant—a holy, lifelong commitment that is not meant to be broken by anything but death. God takes covenant extremely seriously. He gave Himself in covenant to us and backed up His promise with His very life blood. He expects the same from us when we promise to love and cherish our spouses for a lifetime. When arguments arise in your marriage, determine that you will never use the threat of divorce as a weapon against your spouse, no matter how angry or frustrated you are. Decide that you will never insinuate that your marriage is on the verge of collapse. In every conflict, it is vital to have the attitude that you are committed to your marriage no matter what, that you are determined to work through any struggles that threaten your marriage unity. Give your spouse the security of knowing that you intend to honor your marriage covenant for the rest of your days on this earth.

In a Nutshell

If you want to stay madly in love with your spouse through all of life's ups and downs, you're going to need more than a pretty face and a sculpted body. You will need to become a legendary beauty on the *inside*. Bulging muscles on the outside may serve you well in opening a jar of mayonnaise, but sculpted muscles on the *inside* are what enable you to open up the armory of heaven and fight valiantly for marriage intimacy.

Leslie and I refer to this inner nobility as tensile strength. The strength of rope is measured by "tensile strength." Great weights are tied to the rope and then dropped to test the resiliency of the rope under stress. The greater the rope's ability to endure weight and combative force, the stronger the tensile rating. Our hearts are measured for life and marriage the very same way. If we have never focused on building our tensile, then even the smallest weights and stresses will cause us to snap. But if we are willing to build our tensile strength and train like an Olympian, our souls will be able to endure the heaviest, most severe weights life can throw our way.

The ups and downs of married love are too much for a husband and a wife with weak tensile ratings. Marriage brings out a whole host of challenges that a single person can't even comprehend. And the married couple who prove cowardly and weak in the pressure cooker of life's challenges will certainly never reach the glorious heights of married love. A successful marriage necessitates the sculpting and strengthening of our inner lives. In fact, the multitudinous pleasures of married love are discovered in direct proportion to the quality of a married couple's inner physiques.

Chapter Three

HOW TO HAVE AN EXTRAORDINARY SEX LIFE

Marriage isn't about great sex.
Great sex is about a great marriage.

- Eric -

What makes a great lover? A smoldering gaze? Soft caresses? Sultry undergarments? We've all tried to figure out the answer to that question. Growing up, many of us felt the need to master this whole sex thing. Even as third graders we wanted to know what the word *sex* meant. Sex in our culture is like King Kong roaming the streets of Manhattan. Even if you try to act as if the Kong is not at large, the next thing you know a huge ape foot is crashing down upon you.

Sex is everywhere. Sex is the central theme of our modern culture. We feel the immense pressure to have a high sexual-intelligence quotient. We study the sexual moves endorsed by Hollywood. We practice the sexy conversation techniques portrayed by today's hottest TV stars. We try to gain the appeal of *People* magazine's sexiest man alive or *Cosmopolitan*'s latest cover girl. But what most of us fail to realize is that sex in today's culture has become the act of animals rather than the act of a prince and a princess.

We have been led to believe that the more sexually groomed you are prior to marriage, the more capable you will be at the whole sex thing in marriage. That couldn't be farther from the truth. Instead of being great at sex in marriage, most modern couples are just the opposite. Men and women who bring their truckloads of culturally trained sensual experience into marriage are stuck in unhealthy and totally unromantic patterns of sexual interaction that lead only to a shallow, unfulfilling physical experience with their spouses. If you spend your life learning about sex from sitcoms, magazines, peers, and romantically charged movies, the likelihood of your being ready for a great sex life in marriage is about a million to one.

The culture says, "Do what feels good!" And therein lies the root problem. An animal does what "feels good." The culture's motto is "Get yours!" It's selfish, it's greedy, it's crazed, and it's criminal. But since it is so common in our modern world, we applaud it and attempt to emulate its indignity. God is a huge fan of the sexual experience, but He invented sex not as a conduit to depravity, but as a potter's wheel for nobility. Sex is meant to draw out the implanted life of Christ within— to showcase Christ's selfless love more and more throughout a marriage. Sex is meant to be a reminder of heaven, not a lust-filled extravaganza.

Though great sex does feel good, great sex is not about

doing what feels good. Great sex is an act of heroism, nobility, and honor. It's about making your spouse feel good, or maybe I should say making your spouse feel like the most precious and appreciated person in the world. It's about passionately loving your spouse with a sacrificial love—not just in the bedroom, but every moment of the day—with a love that is selfless and surrendering in nature. It's about giving everything you are to another person—laying down your own desires in order to serve and please your spouse. The end result of this sexual other-centeredness is the greatest feeling known to humanity. And God designed it that way. He designed the ultimate act of selflessness to provide the greatest satisfaction.

Sex is euphoric. But the euphoria most couples know is not the complete euphoria that God built into the sex process. It would be ignorant to claim that there is no euphoria in a successful selfish sexual conquest. The world's methods, whereas they are beastly, are not without physical gratification. But the gratification is short-lived and is like a drop of water on a parched desert wanderer's tongue. Never can this drive, this hunger, this appetite be satisfied—because it's an appetite that can be satisfied only by God's means.

Modern sex is a counterfeit of the real thing. Sure, it's pleasurable, but the pleasure lasts only as long as the act itself. And the pleasure seems to dissipate with every subsequent act. Meanwhile, God's version (the real thing) holds more than a mere physical thrill. It also possesses a spiritual and emotional detonation of pleasure that lasts long after the act is completed. It is satisfying at a level human words would fail to properly describe. It's spectacular; it's memorable. And get this: God's rendition of sex only increases in beauty and pleasure throughout married life. It only gets better with time!

Most of us are well-versed in the world's pattern for sexual excellence: A kiss here, a touch there, a caress over here, and then *whamo*—it's time for the really good stuff! If that's your perspective on sex, I'm sorry to burst your bubble, but that's nothing more than a base biological study of human sexuality. Understanding human biology is not without merit, but it shouldn't be the end goal of two spouses enrolled in the school of Christ. We must all become well-versed in *God's* pattern for sexual excellence.

There is more to sex than the right moves and the right timing. There is an art to being a world-class lover in marriage, and shockingly, most of it takes place *outside the bedroom*. To the dismay of many, this chapter is not about moves, erogenous zones, and techniques. (You probably opened the book to this chapter and skipped the first two in the hope of some saucy tidbits on sexual positions. Sorry to disappoint.) This chapter is about something far more important to a couple aiming for the Olympic gold medal in marriage. This chapter is about *how* to have an extraordinary sex life. God invented sex, so let's look at the way He designed it to be fully enjoyed and experienced in marriage.

From a Frog into a Prince

Most of us have spent years being groomed in the animalistic mind-set regarding sex. It's about heat, the urge, and coyote-like yelps in the backseat of an old Ford.

Somehow, this screaming and sweating rendition of sex has caught the fascination of our entire culture. Hollywood fuels this warped mentality. The first thing we must do to understand God's mind-set on sex is to understand His mind-set on all of life. For heavenly nobility to reign, the beast must die. The animal must be caged.

The animal is the surly part of you that craves your way even at the expense of others; it scraps until your every desire is met. If the animal leads the sexual show, then it's curtains on your sex life after only a few months.

A great sex life starts at the very moment the frog begins its transformation into a prince. Amazing sex isn't about mere physical gratification; it's about heaven coming to earth in and through the beauty of two people pouring out their lives for each other in a regal display of the most tender affection this world has ever seen.

Think about the difference between a soldier and a pirate. A soldier and a pirate are both passionate characters that fight and give their lives for a cause. But the difference between the two is one of honor and nobility. A soldier risks his life for others, while a pirate risks his life for his own gain. A pirate is a picture of the animal left uncaged. He plunders the innocent and destroys all that is beautiful for his own amusement and glory. The soldier, on the other hand, is a picture of princely, dignified passion. A soldier devotes his energies and sacrifices personal pleasure in order to give to others, to protect ideals, and to serve all that is beautiful.

Today's lover is 85 percent pirate with 15 percent soldier blended in for the sake of romance. God desires the pirate to walk the plank and the soldier to emerge in all his glory. He knows that the frog must turn into a prince. For the uncaged animal is not just a hindrance to a great sex life in marriage, but also a hindrance to a heaven-reflecting life on earth.

An animal is moved by an urge.	A prince is moved by His God.
An animal is motivated by appetite.	A prince is motivated by a selfless love.
An animal takes what it wants.	A prince gives what another needs most.
An animal wants instant gratification.	A prince is patient for his reward.
An animal is sexually active by instinct.	A prince learns sex as a sacred art of grace.
An animal treats sex as a bodily function.	A prince treats sex as a lifestyle of honor.

Our culture may encourage the animalistic mentality toward sex, but God has a heaven-grown version that trumps Hollywood's most dazzling spectacles. God's version demands a noble mind-set and a regal bearing. It demands a different mentality, a different approach, and a totally different destination. An animal sees sexual climax as the endgame. But a prince sees sexual climax as merely a hallowed moment in the midst of a far greater romantic drama. To a prince and a princess, great sex is the result of a great love shared and cultivated throughout the ebb and flow of daily life. It's not an act; it's a lifestyle. It's not a twenty-minute process from kiss to *whammo*. It's a twenty-four-hour journey from loving sacrifice to loving sacrifice that includes the most incredible *whammo* moments in between. Marriage isn't about great sex. *Great sex is about a great marriage.* When a couple first learn how to be excellent in serving one another, great sex will result naturally whether a couple try for it or not.

Practice Being Royalty

You may be thinking, *Me? Royalty? Ha!* You might feel more comfortable with a burp here, a scratch there, and cheese sauce on your chin than with the polished nobility of the regal life. But it's important to note that if the King of all kings, Jesus Christ, has been implanted into your body, whether you like it or not, the regal life is going to be knocking. A royal bearing doesn't have to mean stiffness. The number one attribute of a royal bearing is *dignity*. And let me forewarn you: burping the alphabet and Christlike dignity don't mix well.

Great sex and dignity go hand in glove. When the animal is caged, the gross beastly behavior patterns are altered to showcase the princely life of Christ. That's when the romantic and sensual beauty of a marriage is ready for liftoff. Dignity means letting Christ harness the wild sexual stallion within, allowing His nature to direct your inner passions so that you give instead of merely take.

Most couples assume that marriage means the inevitable breakdown of romance and beauty. Prior to marriage, there were no piles of dirty clothes, no grotesque burps, and certainly no gaseous clouds hovering overhead during a good-night kiss. Before marriage everything is still beautiful, but once the vows have been exchanged, for some reason couples feel that it's now all about honesty. Sure, marriage is about honesty, but not *that* kind of honesty. Leaving the bathroom door open during the cleansing moments of the day is not a version of honesty that God applauds. Sharing your most intimate burp is not the stuff of lifelong romance. What most modern couples deem "inevitable" is not inevitable at all. If your inner animal is caged and regal manners are cultivated, then marriage can be a theater for the most beautiful displays of human nobility.

A lot of men define masculinity by their ability to gross out all females within a six-mile radius. But when God takes over a man, he redefines manhood to be something noble, princely, warriorlike, poetic, and honorable in every word and action. A man who will be a great lover of his woman is not one who thinks about sex every 3.5 seconds, but one who is passionately dedicated to caring for his princess like the breath in his lungs or the beat of his heart. A man who is great at sex in marriage is one whose mind is consumed with one thing: *showcasing the princely life of Christ to his bride twenty-four hours a day.*

Dignity is not a difficult thing to cultivate. But it does take intentionality. Merely thinking about it doesn't accomplish it. There is the necessity of actually putting it into practice.

Maintaining dignity in a relationship has far more benefits than making a sex life more robust. Life itself is a whole lot more beautiful and fun when dirty clothes aren't strewn over the backs of chairs, when bodily smells are contained to speci-fied closed chambers of the house, and when the mystique of love is preserved.

Become a Student of Your Spouse

Leslie is a girly girl. She loves all the girly stuff, which I, for some reason, have never developed an affinity for: spas, salons, shopping, etc. Not all girls appreciate these things, but believe me, Leslie makes up for all the girls who don't. And I truly treasure this about her. Sure, I may not understand why having her feet soak in hot paraffin wax can make her feel more confident and more beautiful. I may not comprehend why a broken nail is such an egregious affair, but I can say that I'm a blessed man because my wife loves to look beauti-ful for me. She's not obsessed with her looks, and beauty cer-tainly isn't the highest priority of her life, but she puts effort into maintaining her beauty as a gift to her husband.

I want to make my wife feel beautiful. I have learned as Leslie's husband that she subconsciously requires four things to feel beautiful. She needs a beauty budget, private beauty time each day, words from me that affirm her beauty, and possibly most important, my enthusiastic acceptance of this entire "becoming beautiful" process. If I complain about the cost of such beauty maintenance, I instantaneously sabotage the entire process for her. If I infer that her time spent becoming beautiful should be less, then I again undermine her energies in this area. If I gave her money and time but was a scrooge with my verbal affirmation of her beauty, she would probably find herself subconsciously becoming beautiful for someone other than me each day.

Each groom must study his bride to determine what it is she needs to feel beautiful. Every woman is different. Yes, common gender threads do exist, but the role of a great husband is to become a student and figure out the unique qualities of his wife.

I have kept a notebook of my observations of Leslie for years. In this notebook I write down how she thinks, how she feels, what she needs, when she smiles, when she cries, and when she feels most alive. A great sex life flows out of such study. Great sex is, again, not an act. It's the culmination of a thousand loving gestures deftly and tenderly directed toward the love of your life—it's a lifestyle. When a man knows his woman so well that he can begin to anticipate her desires, the sparkle of heaven has come to earth.

Leslie is a very private person. She is modest and mysterious. In fact, one of my favorite attributes of my wife is what I call her mystique. In observing my wife, I decided one day that Leslie would love to have a more guarded private environment in which to become beautiful each day. I moved all my bathroom stuff into the guest-room bath, and we transformed the master bath into "Leslie's Beauty Palace." I painted it for her, and we created a budget so that she could fix it up to be her personal and private sanctuary. Each day she disappears into her personal spa and emerges later a dazzling princess. I don't know what goes on in there. And she won't ever tell me. Her beauty secrets are her own. And as I protect this environment for her and show an enthusiastic support for this process in her life, she only becomes more beautiful and more radiant.

Great sex is not a result of human biology thrown together in the backseat of an old Ford. Great sex is a by-product of two spouses studying each other and learning how the other works and then acting upon that knowledge with enthusiasm and delight. It's a simple principle in our home: when Leslie feels beautiful in the eyes of her groom, she is eager to let her groom know how much she delights in him. And she does this with kisses, caresses, and, ahem . . . you get the idea.

For a woman to be sexually awakened, she needs more than to feel beautiful physically; she also needs to feel cherished inwardly. The results of my eleven years of studying my wife have proved one very important thing to me. Leslie needs to know each day that she is the princess of my heart. She needs to be reminded that she always has access to me, even in the busiest times of work; that she is more important than ministry or making money. Leslie doesn't need diamond earrings to understand this; she needs simple enunciations of my affection packaged into each day. Little notes, unexpected kisses, phone calls in the middle of business meetings, picking up a cup of vanilla chai for her on my way home, or even forsaking a Broncos game to spend the afternoon with her.

A woman is sexually desirous of her husband *in direct proportion to her husband's remembrance of her throughout each day.* A great sex life isn't a difficult science; it's a very practical outflow of the Christ-life within. Guys, treat your woman like a princess each day, and you will be amazed at how much she will desire and enjoy sex.

In the same way I am a student of Leslie, Leslie is a student of me. She knows my points of confidence, and she knows my every insecurity. She understands the inner workings of my manly engine, and she knows what fuel is needed to keep it running strong. She knows that each day I need two basic things. If I have those two basic things, I can tackle any obstacle, I can climb any mountain, I can ford any raging river, and I will be a prince and not a pirate in our relationship throughout the day. So she works diligently to make sure those two things are taken care of each and every day.

1. *I need protected alone time with my God.* I need a heavenly perspective on my day. I need to remember who my source of life is and lean my entire weight afresh upon His almighty arm.

2. *I need the admiration and encouragement of my wife.* I need to know my manhood is appreciated, that my

wife desires me, that she cherishes the unique way in which I am built. I need to hear that I am her hero.

When you are a student of your spouse, you realize that the secret to great sex is treating your spouse like a prince or princess every moment of the day. Loving your spouse this way is not just effective, it is incredibly romantic and fun. But to make it work, the selfish animal within must daily be locked in a cage, and the selfless love life of Christ must be given sway over your existence. Studying your spouse takes time and effort. Learning the regal life takes time and focus. You can't do it in your own strength. But Christ can do it in and through you if you simply allow Him to have His rightful place in your life. So start today—let Christ begin transforming you from a frog into a noble prince (or princess).

Keep the Doors Closed

The sex life of a couple is a supremely private matter. It's supposed to be like the holy of holies in the temple of Jehovah God, a veiled mystery to everyone on the outside. It is not something to share with others; it is something to share only with your spouse. Marriage intimacy is all about an ever-growing depository of secrets kept sacred between a husband and a wife. Things can be shared in this sanctuary of total trust that couldn't possibly be shared anywhere else. The surest way to destroy marriage intimacy is to "kiss and tell."

We've already discussed three key factors that contribute to spectacular lovemaking: (1) allowing Christ to transform you from a frog into a prince or a princess, (2) cultivating royal dignity in your inner life, and (3) becoming a student of your spouse. Now, here's another great-sex necessity: (4) *keep your marriage intimacy sacred*. Proverbs 5:16–17 says, "Should your springs overflow in the streets, your streams of water in the public squares? Let them be yours alone, never to be shared with strangers" (NIV). When the intimate moments of marriage are kept private, they never lose their beauty and are savored for a lifetime.

As Leslie and I speak and write about relationships, it can be tempting to share details from our personal relationship with the world. But Leslie and I decided long ago which aspects of our love story we felt comfortable sharing with others, and which things we were going to hold back for ourselves and never share with anyone. Some years ago we wrote a book about our love story called *When Dreams Come True*.[1] But there are many things about our story that were never written in that book because they are sacred, intimate things meant only for the two of us. The most special memories and moments are the ones we jealously guard and cherish.

Even in writing this chapter on sex, Leslie and I have established very clear parameters on what we will say and will not say about our own intimate life. Guarding privacy isn't something to toy around with in marriage. Leslie and I trust each other implicitly. When we share something in a book, we both agree that it is something we can pass on and that it will not detract from the beauty of what we have together.

Allow your love story to be an encouragement and inspiration to others, but be sure to jealously guard the sacred aspects of your marriage. Don't allow the eyes of the world to peer into your bedroom. Instead, turn it into a marriage sanctuary in which your greatest moments as a couple can unfold. And let the world on the outside only wonder about why you always have a gigantic smile plastered across your face.

Never Stop Winning the Heart

Great effort goes into winning your spouse's heart prior to marriage, but suddenly the vows are spoken, the rings are exchanged, and . . . then what? The final key to unlocking an extraordinary sex life is to *never stop winning the heart of your spouse.* In the same way God never stops pursuing our hearts, we should never stop pursuing our spouses' hearts. Give your spouse every reason to fall in love with you all over again every single day of your life. Instituting a weekly date night is a wonderful idea for any couple. But take it further than that by instituting a constant date *life.* Date your spouse daily, all throughout the day. Don't allow your spouse to slip into the realm of just being your husband or your wife. Maintain the sparkle of romance by making sure he or she remains your lover and your dearest friend.

Many young lovers were full of romantic ideas before the vows were spoken, but now that the honeymoon is over, they suddenly become romantically incompetent. A new husband named Aaron complained, "I have no idea how to keep the romance alive. I've heard that I should 'date my wife,' but I'm not even sure what that means." Ironically, the same romantic tools you may have used to tell your wife of your affection prior to marriage are the same tools that can be used now that you are married. Sunsets, the glimmer of candlelight, love letters, love songs, and creative surprises will still work after the wedding day!

Don't allow the beauty to fade. Don't allow the cares of this world, the responsibilities of life, or even the addition of children to steal away what you share with your lifelong lover. When time is spent making sure your marriage relationship is held sacred, you can be much more effective in every other area of life.

Sex can be great during a honeymoon. It is the long-awaited reward of a couple desperately in love with one another. But honeymoon sex is rookie sex. It's not the result of a lifelong study of another person. Rookie sex is an amazing thing. But, oh, how much more there is to look forward to if you lay the right foundation in these first ninety days of married life together. The intimate sharing of your life with one other person is truly a taste of heaven on earth. And nothing is more amazing or satisfying than heaven!

Here's to making the rest of the world envious!

Putting It into Action

Step #1: Become a One-Woman Man

Now that you have won your spouse's heart, make it your goal to cherish that gift with the way you act in everyday life.

Guys, in order for your bride to give herself fully and completely to you, it is imperative that she knows, without question, that she is the only woman in your heart, your mind, and your dreams. It is a common behavior pattern among modern married males to allow their eyes to wander toward an attractive woman on the street or to drool at the sight of a Victoria's Secret commercial. Instead of looking away or turning the channel, most modern grooms assume that their wives should just accept the fact that they lust after other women. In fact, they get irritated if their wives are disturbed by their insatiable appetite for the bodies of other men's wives.

Our culture has worked overtime convincing us that "men will be men," and that "men have only one thing on their minds." As a result of this twisted message, many men, even Christian men, think it is their "inherent right" to lust after other women, simply because that is the way we are wired as guys. But Christ made His standard for men pretty clear when He said, "Everyone who looks at a woman with lust for her has already committed adultery with her in his heart" (Matthew 5:28 NASB). The Bible says that "there must not be even a hint of sexual immorality, or of any kind of impurity" in our lives (Ephesians 5:3 NIV). Proverbs 5:18–19 tells us to be "captivated" by our wives alone (NIV).

God did not design us as men to covet other women. He created each of us to be a one-woman man. Your wife should be the only woman you dream about, the only woman to whom you give your heart, mind, and body.

If you want to have an amazing sex life as well as a trusting, beautiful marriage, you must become a one-woman man. You have made a covenant before God to give yourself to only one woman for the rest of your life. Now, back that commitment up by guarding your eyes, your mind, and your heart from the perversion of the culture. Anytime you look at or fanaticize about another woman, you undermine the very foundation of your marriage relationship, and you break your wife's heart little by little. So determine now that you will honor your wife at all times by having eyes only for her. Here are some practical ways to make it happen:

Guard Your Mind. Take your thought life seriously. It's not enough to be a one-woman man outwardly; you must be a one-woman man inwardly as well. Self-gratifying thoughts eat away at the foundation of a marriage relationship. Just imagine that your thoughts were projected up on a large movie screen. Would your spouse feel honored by these thoughts, or would she be devastated? Would your thoughts breed confidence in your love for her, or would they undermine the integrity of your marriage? A noble husband seeks to love his wife with his heart, soul, *mind*, and strength.

Unfortunately, modern married men have grown quite accustomed to having lustful, sexually gratifying thoughts milling around in their minds. So cleaning up their thought lives often means a total renovation of their inner environments. If you are like many men today, facing the uphill struggle of overcoming this inner battle of lust, I would strongly recommend that you read my book for men titled *God's Gift to Women: Discovering the Lost Greatness of Masculinity*.[2] Another book that I would highly recommend in relation to overcoming this specific challenge is *Not Even a Hint: Guarding Your Heart Against Lust* by Joshua Harris.[3]

This is serious business in marriage and certainly not a problem to be taken lightly. It's an addiction. And because it's an addiction, it won't disappear with merely a casual desire to quit—it will take a focused effort of the heart and mind. It will take a reformation of basic daily habits, such as what you watch, what you read, how you talk, and how you interact with others.

Like any habit, learning to guard your thought life takes repetition and consistency to become a new behavior pattern in your life. When you are first learning how to guard your mind, there may even be times when you find yourself right back in the mud only a few hours after getting cleaned up. But get back up on that horse, allow God to wash you clean once again, and lean afresh upon His strong arm for help in this superimportant battle. If you are consistent in your efforts to fight against self-ish and sensually hazardous thoughts, then in due time it will become habitual to keep your mind set apart for your wife.

Guard Your Eyes. Sexual temptation is all around us in today's culture. But that doesn't mean we are helpless against it any more than we are helpless against eating junk food. We can choose to *look away* when temptation comes. When a Hooter's billboard screams for your attention, keep your eyes on the road in front of you. When seductive magazines at the checkout stand try to grab your view, study the gum selection instead. And when a scantily dressed woman saunters by, do not follow her with your eyes.

And just as with guarding your thoughts, guarding your eyes will often mean establishing new behavior patterns. New habits will need to be formed in order to fortify your marriage relationship—habits that bless rather than hurt. A man who guards his gaze is a man who loves his woman. If your wife knows that you have eyes only for her, she will also have the confidence of knowing that she is the only one who holds your heart and your mind.

Be Accountable. If you are struggling with lust, it is wise to have at least one other Christian man to whom you can be accountable. Find someone—whether it be a pastor, a spiritual leader, or a trusted friend—in whom you can confide and who will provide you with prayer and exhortation as you seek to become a one-woman man. Make sure it is a person who will keep you accountable to your marriage covenant, someone who will challenge you to rise to the holy standard of Christ. If your chosen accountability partner proclaims, "Dude, men are men! Don't feel guilty about the way you are wired!" then find someone else. Do whatever it takes to be set apart for your wife, even if you must get uncomfortable and make major changes in your life and attitude.

Write Out Your Commitment. Sometimes it can help in being set apart to write out your commitment to remain mentally, physically, and emotionally loyal to your wife. This statement of faithfulness could be simply a rewrite of your wedding vows, a love letter written to your bride, a written prayer to God, or a code of conduct that you use as a reminder to yourself. Be as specific as possible. Talk about your decision to protect your mind and to honor your wife with your body, your thoughts, and your attitude. Put your written commitment in a place where you can see it often and be reminded that you are a one-woman man.

- Leslie -

Step #2: Become a One-Man Woman

Ladies, make up your mind once and for all that you are a one-man woman. You have made a covenant before God to give yourself to only one man for the rest of your life—your husband. There is no room for exception. And just as before marriage it was important to set clear boundaries to protect your purity, now that you are married it's important to adopt a clear battle plan for protecting your marriage covenant. Throughout your life, there may be many temptations to let down your guard; to become lazy and apathetic in setting your life apart for your husband. Commitment and faithfulness must be fought for and protected. Here are some practical ways to craft your battle plan.

Guard Your Mind. Decide that you will never allow yourself to daydream or fantasize about another man—whether he's real or imagined. If watching certain movies or reading certain kinds of books causes you to become discontented with your husband and tempts your mind to dream about a steamy romance with an imaginary hunk, then remove those things from your life. Many a wife has become disgruntled with her husband and emotionally attached to a fictional lover through reading romance novels. Be just as vigilant about real-life temptations. If spending time around a certain man is causing you to daydream or fantasize about him romantically, then go out of your way to avoid that person (yes, even if he is a friend—that friendship is not worth jeopardizing your marriage). And the moment a thought enters your mind that is dishonoring to your husband, train your mind to immediately "kick it out" by praying for an unsaved friend, meditating on Scripture, or dwelling on all the good qualities your husband has.

Guard Your Body. Your body is for your husband's enjoyment—not for the enjoyment of any other man. Modesty is just as important for a woman after marriage as it is prior to marriage. Make sure you aren't dressing in a way that would tempt other men to lust over your body. This doesn't mean you need to wear drab, shapeless clothes; dress attractively, but also in a way that honors your husband. Don't give other men previews of what only your husband is meant to see! If you are unsure what is appropriate, spend some time seeking God's direction, and ask your husband for his input.

Every woman must decide individually before God what kind of clothes are honoring to Him and to her spouse. But for what it is worth, here are some of the guidelines that have helped *me* in choosing clothes that honor Eric:

- Wear clothes that draw attention upward toward the face, not downward toward the body. (For example, if you follow the lines of a low-cut top, they point toward the chest like an arrow.)

- Avoid clothes that are too tight. My rule of thumb is that if something is too tight to easily move around in, then it is probably too tight to be appropriate.

- Avoid clothes that give "peeks" (e.g., tops that flop open when you lean over, shirts that show your stomach when you lift your arms, and super-low-cut pants that show skin whenever you bend down).

- Avoid clothes that specifically draw attention to inappropriate areas—such as shirts that have strategically positioned graphics across the chest and pants that have attention-grabbing writing or graphics across the seat.

- And while you are guarding your body for your husband, be aware of the way you walk, stand, sit, etc. Make sure that seductive movements are saved for your husband alone and not used for the visual pleasure of other men.

Write Out Your Commitment. Sometimes it can help in being set apart to write out your commitment to remain mentally, physically, and emotionally loyal to your husband. This statement of faithfulness could be simply a rewrite of your wedding vows, a love letter written to your groom, a written prayer to God, or a code of conduct that you use as a reminder to yourself. Be as specific as possible. Talk about your decision to protect your mind and to honor your husband with your body, your thoughts, and your attitude. Put your written commitment in a place where you can see it often and be reminded that you are a one-man woman.

Step #3: Study and Serve Your Spouse

As Eric mentioned earlier, he keeps a notebook of observations about me that he calls "studying womanhood." By taking the time to observe me, he knows how to serve me best. He understands how to win and warm my heart. He knows that little reminders of his love mean the world to me. So every few days, he writes me a little love note or expresses his appreciation for my life. He has observed that I become stressed when the house is a mess. So whenever he has a spare moment, he cleans up without my having to ask him. I have also observed him over the years. I have realized that when he is starting to feel discouraged, getting out of the house, drinking a cup of chai, and talking about where our life is headed will refresh and uplift him. I know that when he has too much on his plate, he needs me to help him get organized and prioritize his tasks. The more we study each other, the more we learn how to serve each other according to our specific needs.

In order to really serve someone, you must observe his or her life and learn what makes him or her tick. You might think that your wife's day would be made by giving her flowers, when what she would *really* like is for you to clean the house without being asked. You might assume that your husband would love a night out with the guys, when what he would *really* love is for you to surprise him with a romantic getaway to your favorite hotel. Consider starting a notebook of observations about your spouse. Every time you learn something about what makes him or her come to life, write down your observations in the notebook. Each time you realize what hurts him or her, write down those things as well. From time to time, read through your notes and remind yourself how your spouse ticks.

The more you study your spouse and go out of your way to serve him or her in specific ways, the more your sex life—as well as your intimacy and friendship—will sparkle. Remember, self-lessness is the secret to extraordinary sex—selflessness that takes place not just in the bedroom, but in day-to-day life as well. Selflessness means getting outside of your own skin and looking at life from the other person's perspective. As you study and serve your spouse, you will learn more and more to love as Christ loves.

Step #4: Develop Daily Romance Rituals

Every night before we drift off to sleep, Eric tells me that he loves me and that I am the greatest wife in the world. Every morning before we start the day, I give Eric a long hug and tell him that he is my hero. We don't say these words out of duty or obligation, but out of genuine love and commitment to each other. Little expressions like these keep our romance fresh and our appreciation for each other in the forefront of our minds.

Don't save special words of love and appreciation for Valentine's cards once a year. Don't keep tender touches of affection only for times of physical intimacy. Adopt daily romance rituals that constantly remind each other of your love and devotion. Take some time to develop your own daily romance ritual. It doesn't have to be anything elaborate—just a little reminder of your love and commitment. Don't assume that just because you told your wife you loved her two months ago, she doesn't need to hear it constantly. And don't think that just because you told your husband you admired him last year, he wouldn't love to hear those words every single day. Be *generous* with your expressions of love and with the little reminders of your affection, and the beauty of your marriage will shine brighter each and every day.

Step #5: Guard Dignity in Everyday Life

Many modern couples think that marriage is the time when you can finally "let it all hang out." There are plenty of jokes about men who burp, scratch, and pack on the pounds, and women who stop shaving their legs or wearing makeup once the wedding vows are spoken. And sadly, it is all too true. There is a common assumption that once you have "locked in" your spouse's commitment to you, you no longer need to work to win his or her heart—that you can now be sloppy and careless and throw dignity to the wind. But not only does this attitude show an incredible lack of respect for your spouse; it is a sure recipe for a mediocre sex life.

Does a woman's heart pound with desire for a man who is lounging on the couch eating greasy junk food, loudly burping, and emitting foul odors into the air? Is a man turned on by a sloppy, haggard woman who doesn't give the time of day to her appearance? Don't let marriage be an excuse to stop putting effort into your behavior or appearance. Giving attention to how you look only before you go out in public but not when you are home alone with your husband sends the message that he is less important to you than a stranger at the mall. Thinking about being socially polished only when you are around others shows your wife that you don't value her as much as you do your friends.

Now that you have won your spouse's heart, make it your goal to *cherish* that gift with the way you act in everyday life. Take some time to develop a "code of conduct" for the way you will behave around each other now that you are married. Determine now that you will always treat each other with dignity and respect. Manners and social courtesy are just as important after marriage as they are before marriage. Guarding dignity in everyday life will go a long way to preserve the beauty of your romance and the passion in your sex life. Here are some practical ways to make it happen:

Maintain Individual Privacy. It is true that marriage is a total openness, a complete giving of everything when it comes to your heart and life. But as Eric discussed earlier, there are some things in marriage that are better *not* shared with your spouse. There is no reason to leave the bathroom door open so your spouse can observe you answering nature's call. In fact, it's a show of disrespect not to be more considerate. When it comes to basic human dignity, privacy is something that is best guarded in a marriage. It's even a good idea to have separate bathrooms if at all possible. And if not, then at least maintain your individual privacy when it comes to the less-dignified things in life. Of course, there may be times when this is impossible. When I was in labor with our son, there wasn't much I could do to maintain my privacy *or* dignity.

Eric stayed right by my side, serving me and loving me even when I had very little beauty, modesty, or dignity, and this actually strengthened our marriage relationship. In your marriage, there might be times of sickness or other circumstances in which privacy is thrown to the wind—and that is certainly okay. But in everyday life, show respect to each other by keeping personal bodily functions as private as possible.

Maintain Social Grace. When you are at church or having dinner with your business associates, you are (hopefully) careful not to belch, emit foul odors into the air, talk with your mouth full, or pick your nose. This is because you have social grace. You treat people with politeness because you want them to know they are valued. You might not worry about your behavior or manners around a dog, but people are a different story. Even strangers are worthy of your basic respect; they are worth the effort you make to keep your behavior polished instead of gross.

Your spouse is no less worthy of your respect when it comes to basic social behavior. Yet in modern marriages too many couples throw away all social grace the moment the honeymoon is over, or sometimes even sooner. If you want to preserve the mystery and romance of your marriage, a great way to start is by preserving basic social grace. Make up your mind that you will not use marriage as an excuse to act like a Neanderthal. Treat each other with the same social respect you would your church friends or business friends. This doesn't mean you have to be stiff and uncomfortable around each other, worried about every little thing you do or say. You should feel the freedom to be totally relaxed around each other *while maintaining basic social dignity*. You don't have to burp, scratch, pick, etc., in order to be comfortable around your spouse. Save the "gross" things for private moments—or, if possible, eliminate them altogether! Honor your spouse by maintaining basic social grace in his or her presence, and the mystery of your romance will be preserved.

Maintain Your Appearance. Physical appearance is another area that is all too often thrown to the wind not long after the wedding vows are spoken. Men and women who gave careful attention to their appearance before marriage suddenly become sloppy and careless when it comes to taking care of their bodies. They might make an effort to look presentable when going out in public, but in their own homes they roll out of bed, throw on a dirty T-shirt, and waddle down the stairs to begin the day, without so much as a glance in the mirror. As mentioned earlier, Eric and I decided early in our marriage that we wanted to honor each other by taking care of our bodies. We watch what we eat, exercise regularly, and give attention to basic grooming—even when it is just the two of us at home alone. This doesn't mean we're obsessed with how we look. There are plenty of times (like first thing in the morning or when we are sick) when we see each other looking our worst, and this doesn't affect our love or commitment to each other. But as much as possible, we try to honor each other by taking care of our appearance. It's not something we do out of paranoia; it's a special gift we delight in giving each other. And after eleven years of marriage, Eric still turns my head when he walks into a room—and I turn his. A great way to preserve the mystery and passion of your sex life is to take care of your body as a gift to your spouse. It shouldn't be something that you stress about, just something that you factor into your daily routine as a sign of honor and respect for the one you love.

In a Nutshell

Great sex is not an act; it's a lifestyle. And it's not the fruition of a primal urge, but the evidence of a romantic God. Great sex is not found in marriage by following a sexual appetite, but through being led by a selfless love.

Modern couples, raised on Hollywood's rendition of sex, take into marriage a truckload of bizarre misconceptions and twisted mentalities. But in modeling the self-gratifying, animalistic methods of this culture, you are sabotaging your sex life before it even begins. God invented sex. Who better to define how it can be maximized in our lives?

Great sex is not the work of animals. Animals may have sex, but it's certainly not great sex. Great sex is reserved for those made in the image of God—for those who can understand its regal nature and utilize sexuality as the ultimate expression of love. God designed sex to be a sacred art of grace, practiced by a prince and a princess. Great sex is found not in taking, but in giving. It's not a bodily function, but a lifestyle of love and honor.

If your inner animal is caged and regal manners are cultivated, then marriage can be a theater for the greatest sex imaginable, a demonstration of one of the most beautiful displays of Christlike nobility.

Chapter Four

HOW TO TACKLE LIFE
AS A TEAM

> *Great marriage is the forging of two destinies for a common purpose.*

- Eric -

I was stuck in a basement room the other day for a very long two and a half hours with a group of unsavory men. The common interest that brought us all together was football. I like football a lot, but as a result of my football fetish, I sometimes find myself in what I call "burper-scratcher hell." And this past Sunday afternoon, thanks to a misguided invitation and an awkward moment, I once again stumbled into a gladiators' arena laden with the sounds of belching, beer guzzling, and beastly behavior. Sure, in our modern world I could just shrug my shoulders and say, "That's just the way guys are." Honestly, it wouldn't even bother me if these guys also didn't claim to be Christian men.

Call me an idealist, but I have higher expectations for men who claim to know Christ. I certainly don't expect perfection of anyone, but I do expect a certain measure of nobility. I like hanging out with guys, and I'm able to look past a lot of these evidences of modern male mediocrity and still enjoy their company. But I must admit, it aggravates me when I see "Christian" men treat their wives and children as if they are less important than their own personal agendas.

"Craig," one wife began during the game, peeking her head around the corner into the gladiators' arena, "can Tyson come down and watch the game with you?"

"No!" Craig responded in a demeaning tone. "I can't watch a game and watch a two-year-old at the same time!"

"He really wants his daddy, Craig!" the wife pleaded.

"Kara, you take care of him! He's not coming down here and ruining the game for me!"

It's *that* attitude that bothers me. It's as if Craig thinks because he is a man he is entitled to his fun, his way, his peace, his quiet, and his football.

Another wife dared to come down the stairs and speak. "Jeff, how much longer is this game going to last?"

"Brenda!" Jeff moaned in disgust. "It's a football game. It's over when it's over!"

Seeing this all-too-familiar scenario, the guys around me let out a stifled chuckle. They, too, were well acquainted with the nagging wife and the needy kids who were always trying to sabotage their guy time. They knew their wives upstairs were all wondering the same thing Brenda was, but Brenda was the only one bold enough to actually speak it.

For two and a half hours I endured this masculine show of power. The belches, the beer guzzling, and the beastly behavior started to really get under my skin. Guy power feeds on a pack mentality. One guy alone in front of a TV football game can certainly be a display of chauvinism, but jam ten of them together in a basement room in front of a Broncos game, and it's simply disgraceful. I found myself leaving early, even before the game was over, simply to keep from bursting a blood vessel.

What upsets me is that these men claim their behavior is backed by the Bible. They believe Scripture endorses this selfish behavior by stating the husband is the "head" of the household. These men have taken a powerful biblical truth of manhood and somehow twisted it into a disastrous display of self-centeredness.

The concept of "headship" is a tremendous truth, but it means something far different from what most modern men think it does. The head of the marriage relationship isn't free to do whatever he wants. Rather, he is the one who *surrenders* his freedoms to make sure his household is protected and cared for. The head is not the position of ease, but the position of greatest responsibility and heaviest workload. The husband should be the one to initiate, to serve first, to give first, to seek forgiveness first, to pursue spiritual growth first, and to lay down his very life for the lives of his bride and his children.

Marriage isn't only about the husband and his agenda. Marriage is about the forging of two destinies for a common purpose. Marriage is about a bride just as much as it is about a groom. And if a groom ignores all that the bride offers the relationship, the relationship will always remain mediocre, and the husband will always be a mediocre man.

Marriage is about selfless servanthood. It's true that a great wife abandons her life to serve her man in marriage. But a great husband abandons *his* life to serve his wife, as Christ did for us, His bride.

A great marriage isn't about Craig and Jeff sitting in their Barcaloungers burping and scratching and commanding their wives to submit to their every pleasure. A great marriage is about Craig and Jeff forgoing their own desires and pursuits. It's about Craig and Jeff actually *serving* their wives and children and showcasing to them the extraordinary love of Christ.

"Craig, Tyson really needs his daddy right now!"

The challenge comes to each of us as men. We all might not be named Craig, but we all recognize the test. It's those moments when what is truly important (i.e., relationships) clashes with our selfish pleasures (e.g., football). These are the moments that define our manhood, that prove our substance as husbands and as fathers.

If we say, "No! I can't watch the game and watch a two-year-old at the same time!" what we are really saying is, "Kara, you must realize that my personal agenda is more important than my wife and my son."

I'll forewarn you now, guys, that attitude is a sure way to end up sleeping on the couch . . . *permanently*. It is also a sure way to undermine the intimacy of marriage, and therefore your communication and your collective vision as a couple.

"Jeff, how much longer is that football game going to last?"

Yes, to a self-centered man, those words could be construed as nagging. But to a man who is truly "the head of his home," those are words that should prick the knight within him to rise up and be noble. Those are words that should cause a man to recalibrate his priorities to ensure that, even above his own personal pleasure, his wife and children are attended to.

Marriage is about a man and a wife becoming the ultimate team. It's not just about the wife serving her husband or the husband serving his wife; it's about both of them serving each other simultaneously. A great husband is one who knows how to bend his knee and wash his bride's feet. And a great wife is one who knows how to sacrificially shape her husband into a prince. A great team is one in which both members work in harmony with each other, always making sure the team is unified and headed in the exact same direction. A great team is one in which each member is constantly watchful of the other's needs and eager to help meet them. The members of a great team make decisions together and never independently of each other. A great team *shares* the weighty responsibilities of life. A great team, if built well, can carry a marriage through the harshest struggles, the most extreme crises, and the hottest trials.

Marriage is the ultimate team sport. If you want your new life as a married couple to really *work*, functioning as a team is essential. Modern culture often creates couples who live two separate lives but just happen to share a bed. The man goes off to a job that his wife doesn't really understand, and the woman spends time on things that her husband doesn't appreciate or value. The man has "his" car, and the woman has "her" money. But in God's design, a couple's life together was meant to be shared fully and completely—not *yours and mine*, but *ours*. From finances to career pursuits to household chores to raising kids, true success will be found only when you learn to tackle these things together.

Leslie and I are a team. We do everything as if in harmony. That harmony doesn't naturally always occur. There are times when it takes a lot of work to find that place of agreement, but nonetheless, Leslie and I never move forward in anything in our life together without a mutual nod of consent. As the husband, I may be the head of our home, but that doesn't mean I run our home according to my personal agenda and force my wife into subservience. Rather, as the "head," I am responsible to make sure that my wife is understood and that her thoughts are heard and validated. As the head, I am responsible for drawing my wife out and fully appreciating all that she is capable of bringing to our marriage. As the head of our home, I am her prince, her greatest advocate, and her most reliable confidant.

The Prince of the Home

Being the head of the home carries with it a great challenge. Most men would not claim to be the head if they really knew what it meant. It takes a real man to carry such a heavy weight and to bend to such a level of servant-hearted humility. And God designed us as men to carry out such a noble role.

As the head, a man carries the responsibility for protecting his marriage and his home. Being the head isn't license for a man to be selfish. Instead, it's a heavenly burden to make absolutely sure that the supremacy of Christ is maintained in every corner of his marriage and family. Being the head isn't a husband's excuse for slovenly behavior, but a commission from the King of all kings to discipline his life around God's heavenly agenda. It is the husband's role to model Christ and inspire his wife and children toward the brilliance of Jesus. To do this, we must be willing to take the most extreme measures necessary.

Guys, whatever stands in the way of your showcasing the servant heart of Christ in your home must be eliminated. For instance, if watching football is a hindrance to the integrity and harmony of your home, then the television should be turned off. If your career pursuits are creating unhealthy spiritual growth patterns in your family, then you should find a new line of work. If something even as small as reading the newspaper in the morning is distracting you from addressing the real issues taking place inside your home, then the paper should be tossed in the trash.

Taking Responsibility

The man is the prince of the home. And because you are the prince, the buck stops with you. As the husband, you are ultimately responsible for all the moral and ethical decisions you and your wife make together. You must answer to heaven for the spiritual and moral management of your home. As the head, you must answer to God Himself for the character of your marriage and the substance of your home. If a marriage decision cannot be agreed on by you and your wife, the man must be the one to decide. You must be the final arbiter, for you are also the one ultimately responsible for the decision before God. However, the need for the man to be the "final arbiter" is a very rare instance in a healthy marriage. After eleven years of marriage, I have never made a major decision as the head of our home that Leslie hadn't already checked off on. This isn't to say circumstances couldn't arise that would demand a man to make a difficult decision that is not a unified one; it's just to say it should be the rare exception and certainly not the rule.

Championing Your Wife's Future

As the prince of the home, the man holds the privileged position of being the champion of his wife's future. Far too many men today limit the potential of their wives. They mentally fence in a woman's potential impact and subconsciously assume that a godly woman can be nothing more than a wife and a mother. A great husband learns to catch *God's* vision for his wife's life. A Christ-built husband seeks to empower and enable his wife the very way Christ seeks to empower and enable His bride. He becomes a champion for her life, studying her, cheering her on, helping shape her into a world-impacting princess.

Leslie is an astounding wife and mother. I deeply cherish how she loves me, serves me, cares for me, admires me, and helps me run my unique spiritual race. I deeply appreciate how she loves our son and pours out her life to see him grow in grace. However, Leslie is far more than just a wife and a mother. Anyone who knows her instantly recognizes the fire burning in her eyes. She is designed by the Almighty to impact this world for Him. She aches for a lost world. She is a talented communicator, an accomplished artist with the brush of truth. It is my great delight as her husband to fully appreciate these qualities and fan them into flame within her life.

I make room in our schedule for her to grow her ministry to young, set-apart women. I protect her time at the piano so she can create music that makes God smile. I encourage and assist her when she writes a life-changing book. I am awed when I see her impact on this culture. I don't feel threatened by her life and her influence . . . *I treasure it.* I am her biggest fan. Leslie doesn't aspire to center stage. She doesn't try to claim the head position in our home. She is merely a woman functioning the way God built her to function, secure in her God's and her husband's adoring love and approval.

A man is the prince of the home, and, therefore, he holds the noble role of laying down his life for his bride. Guys, don't fear that in doing this you will lose your masculinity. A woman loved with such a sacrificial manly love can't help but admire and respect a man who resembles Christ in so many profound ways. A man who bears nail wounds on behalf of his beloved bride is the warrior-poet of every woman's dreams.

- Leslie -

The Princess of the Home

In the movie *My Big Fat Greek Wedding,* a seasoned wife shares a "marital secret" with her daughter: "A man may be the head of the home, but the woman is the neck, and she can turn the head any way she wants." That comical statement is a rather pompous exaggeration of a very real truth: women wield a tremendous power over their husbands' lives. Our words, attitudes, and actions can either shape our men into noble princes or tear them down to wimpy schmucks. Ladies, God has given you the ability to influence your man in a way that no other person on earth can. The question is, will you use your position for good or for harm in your husband's life?

It's easy to use our feminine power to manipulate, control, and nag our husbands into serving our own selfish agendas. When we see our husbands' less-than-Christlike qualities, it's tempting to point them out and complain about them. When our husbands adopt the mediocre standards of today's men, it's easy to throw up our hands in disgust and rant about the many shortcomings of the male species. But manipulation and complaining don't make a wife into a princess. And they certainly don't make a husband into a noble prince.

A true princess has heavenly eyes for her man. She believes in him, she applauds his hard work, and she is his biggest fan in the world. To be a great husband, a man desperately needs a great wife. His strength and confidence hinge upon her admiration and emotional support. The more of Christ a wife shows to her husband on a daily basis, the more his impact will be upon the world each and every day. And even when it seems her man isn't responding to her efforts, a true princess continues to spur him on toward greatness with her selfless love and devotion.

When Eric and I were married eleven years ago, we had a foot-washing ceremony in our wedding. We tenderly washed each other's feet as a statement that we intended to pour out our lives for each other just as Christ had poured out His life for us. We were committing to serve each other selflessly, following in the sacrificial footsteps of our Lord. During my part of the foot-washing, a song played that I had written and recorded for Eric. It declared my desire to be his devoted servant, to lay down my own dreams and plans and pour my life into his. After the wedding, I received criticism from some wives who thought my expression of servanthood was a little too extreme. "I don't think you need to refer to yourself as Eric's *servant*," said one woman. "It sounds so demeaning. You aren't his slave, you know. You still have your own life." Other women agreed. "I think you are taking it too far," they told me. "Of course you want to help him and honor him, but a wife doesn't need to grovel at her husband's feet."

I understood why these women were concerned about my desire to be Eric's servant. There is a common attitude among modern wives that says we must stand up for ourselves—to make sure our husbands never take us for granted, to make sure we are receiving just as much as we are giving. We fear that the moment we choose to give up the control position in our marriages, we have signed away our lives and our identities. We think if we humble ourselves to serve our husbands, we will lose our respect and dignity as women and become nothing but doormats. But, as a great Christian woman once said, "Christ became even *lower* than a doormat." Christ did not scrape and grasp for His rights, His power, or His control. He willingly sacrificed them in order to meet our greatest needs. There is no greater lover than the One who stooped so low and sacrificed so much for the sake of His beloved. Christ was not worried about what He would receive from us. He simply gave—He willingly poured out His breath and blood because He loved us (see Philemon 2:6–8).

As the princesses of our homes, we are called to love our husbands this way. Not holding back, but pouring ourselves out for our men with abandon. Not scraping for our own rights, not grasping for our own agendas, but humbling ourselves daily, seeking our spouses' good above our own.

Being a Christlike servant to your husband does not mean that you have no voice, no opinion, and no identity. But you should not be consumed with protecting those things. Instead, you should be consumed with showcasing the nature of Christ to your man. A true princess is both a gentle breeze and a mighty rock in her husband's life. As the princess of your home, you provide refreshment, encouragement, and tenderness when your husband is weary from life's battles. And you offer strength, exhortation, and words of inspiration when he needs to be motivated toward greatness.

In eleven years of marriage, I have not always selflessly served Eric—far from it. Many times my own agenda has taken over. At times I have chosen to nag and manipulate rather than uplift and encourage. But my original commitment to be Eric's servant has remained unchanged. And through Christ's supernatural enabling power, I have been shaped more and more into the princess of our home. And ironically, as I learn to selflessly pour out my life for my husband, I don't lose my dignity and respect. In fact, just the opposite happens. As I pour my life out for him, Eric only respects me more. I haven't become a doormat under Eric's feet. He is always looking for ways to pour out his life for me in return.

Being the princess of the home is anything but a position of weakness. Loving like Christ is not insignificant and demeaning—it is eternal and ennobling. As the line from *My Big Fat Greek Wedding* goes, "A man may be the head of the home, but the woman is the neck." The neck is what supports the head; it's what gives the head strength to function as it was meant to function. Ladies, use your powerful position to uplift and strengthen your prince rather than serve your own agenda, and you will see the warrior-poet of your dreams emerge before your eyes.

Unity is a powerful thing. It's worth protecting, and it's worth fighting for. But unity in marriage demands that each spouse learn to serve and learn to sacrifice. Unity demands that both spouses study intensely to become experts on each other's lives. Marriage isn't about a husband, and marriage isn't about a wife. Marriage is about a husband and a wife joined together by God to accomplish far more as a team than either one possibly could alone.

Here's to growing old and gray together!

Putting It into Action

Step #1: Grow Together Spiritually

If you and your spouse work together to conquer the daily tasks of life, you will experience a level of success and fulfillment most modern couples only dream of.

To remain a strong team throughout your marriage, one of the most important things you can do is grow together spiritually. While it is certainly important to have your own individual relationships with God, there is now a new dimension to your spiritual life: your relationship with God *as a couple*. When one spouse moves forward spiritually and the other remains spiritually stagnant, the marriage team is compromised. A figure-skating team cannot be excellent together if one partner is at the Olympic level and the other is still learning how to skate backward. The beauty of a fully functioning marriage team is experienced only when both members pursue spiritual excellence *together*. This is what the apostle Paul meant when he said that Christian marriages should not be "unequally yoked" (2 Corinthians 6:14 NKJV).

Together, you can have a far greater spiritual impact for God's kingdom than you can apart. But becoming a spiritual team, being "equally yoked," takes focus and effort. Modern Christianity does not always make it easy for couples to grow together spiritually. There are women's Bible study groups and men's prayer meetings, men's rallies and women's conferences, spiritual-growth books for men and different books for women.

And while being strengthened spiritually from a male-only or female-only perspective can be important and healthy, it should never replace being strengthened spiritually as a team. Here are some practical ways to make sure you are growing together spiritually.

Explore God's Word Together. Plan a time in your schedules, whether daily or weekly, when you can sit down together and study God's Word as a couple. Discuss ahead of time what areas of the Bible you would like to learn more about, and then be sure to obtain all the necessary tools ahead of time that will help you have an effective study session. There are many great resources to help you get started in a joint Bible study journey. (As a starting place, Eric and I recommend the Bible studies available at www.precept.org and Howard Hendricks's *Living by the Book*.[1]) At first, studying the Bible together may not seem a very exciting way to spend your time. But as you pursue God's Word together, you will discover rich spiritual truths that will greatly enhance your lifestyle and your relationship with God and each other. You will naturally become more and more of a unified team, sharing the same vision, passion, convictions, and beliefs. If you develop this habit early in your marriage, you will be amazed at the lifelong benefits it will reap.

Pray and Worship Together. If you haven't already developed the daily habit of praying with your spouse, then begin tonight.

Praying together daily for your life and marriage reminds you to keep Christ in the center of your relationship. It helps you realize that you can do nothing in your own strength, and it keeps you dependent upon God as a couple. Eric and I pray together every night before we go to bed—we thank God for the day and lay all of our "burdens" at His feet. Each morning, as soon as we wake up, we hold hands and offer ourselves fully and completely to God, yielding to Him afresh and allowing Him to do whatever He desires in and through us that day.

Agreeing together in prayer is one of the single greatest ways to establish unity in your marriage relationship. It may feel awkward to pray aloud together if you have never done it before, but if you begin to carve out time for prayer together each day, it will soon become a natural part of your life. Eric and I also love to worship together—to sit at the piano and sing songs of love to our Lord. Focusing on Christ as a couple is a wonderful way to take your eyes off self and circumstances and remember what a huge, amazing God you serve. Consider taking time to worship with your spouse—whether you plunk out songs on your guitar, listen to a worship CD, or simply read a psalm out loud. The more you turn your eyes to heavenly things together, the more you will naturally be on the same page through the ups and downs of life.

Read Spiritual Books Together. Eric and I have found that reading spiritual books as a couple—especially historical Christian biographies—greatly inspires us to grow together spiritually.

Even before we were married, we read books about heroic Christians and discussed our desire to emulate their examples. Reading stories of great Christians as a couple offers many hours of significant discussion—talking about their lives of sacrifice and wondering if and how God might use us in the same way. Books like these help paint a picture of the amazing adventure God has called us to as a couple—and help remind us never to settle for spiritual mediocrity. Take some time to obtain a few biographies of Christian men and women—then read them out loud together and talk about their lives. (A list of books that Eric and I have found extremely inspiring can be found on our Web site, www.whenGodwrites.com.)

Attend Christian Events Together. Whenever possible, attend Christian events—such as conferences or retreats—together rather than separately. Christian events are often places where we have "mountaintop experiences" with God—they provide times to get away from the daily routine of life and be spiritually renewed and refreshed. It is difficult to share the depth of your experience with your spouse if he or she has not been a part of what has taken place. If you return from a Christian event motivated and spiritually charged, and your spouse is in the same place he or she was before you left, unable to comprehend what you are so excited about, it can cause a great deal of frustration and even marital friction. But if you experience the mountaintop together, you will be much more able to implement your new understanding of truth into your daily life as a unified team.

This isn't to say that attending Christian events separately is harmful—sometimes it can be very refreshing to get away on your own and spend time learning more about God's ways as an individual. But when you do, be sure that you plan a time to sit down with your spouse and allow him or her to share in what you learned and experienced there. Offer plenty of grace if your spouse doesn't fully appreciate your excitement—remember that your spouse has been plugging away in the typical daily grind while you have been on the mountaintop. No matter what the response, do your best to let your spouse be a part of all that God is doing in your life, rather than hording the "treasures" all for yourself.

Share What You Are Learning Individually. Even as you grow together spiritually, it is important that you each maintain your individual relationships with God. Eric has an extremely passionate and active spiritual life, and I had to learn early in our marriage that I could not live *my* spiritual life vicariously through his. I needed to keep pursuing my own passionate relationship with Christ. We make our own individual quiet times a top priority in our life together. And when God is at work in my heart, I share it with Eric. When I feel a specific nudge in a certain direction or I feel convicted about heading down the wrong path, I make sure that I tell Eric what is going on inside me. And when I uncover an exciting truth in Scripture or read an incredible testimony of faith in a Christian biography, I share my discoveries with my husband. He does the same for me. We don't share every little nuance about our individual spiritual lives, but we do make an effort to keep each other aware of and involved in what is happening spiritually in our hearts and minds. The more you learn to talk about spiritual things and discuss how God is working in you, the more your individual spiritual lives will flow in the same direction.

- Eric -

The Importance of Men Taking the Spiritual Lead. As I said earlier in this chapter, men are designed by God to be the initiators and the protectors within a relationship. But this role isn't supposed to be isolated to merely asking your girl to dance or making the proposal. It applies first and foremost to the spiritual dimension of your married life. A lot of men struggle with taking the initiative and being the protector in the spiritual side of the marriage. For many guys, it's the equivalent of admitting to bed-wetting when they were eight to say to their wives, "Darling, I think we should spend some time praying about this decision."

Guys, if you haven't talked about spiritual things much in your life leading up to your marriage, it will be strange to take the spiritual lead. It might be awkward at first, like learning how to drive with a clutch or learning how to eat with braces. It will take some time, but if you keep trying, soon it will feel like second nature. And girls, be patient with your man. Encourage and inspire him, and don't manipulate him or make him feel guilty because of his slow development or the awkwardness he may feel in this area.

The spiritual dimension in life is the bedrock of great romance. And it must be treated as the most important thing in your marriage and home. As a guy, if you are looking for something to protect, something to fight for, and something to die for, look no farther than the spiritual climate of your home.

Encourage your wife to spend time with God. Initiate spiritual discussions in your private time together. Take seriously the church environment that you and your family are a part of— test it, evaluate it, question it, and make sure it is the very best place for your marriage and family to grow healthy and strong.

Guys, if you didn't have a dad who modeled a spiritual leader and you are struggling to know exactly what you are supposed to be doing, then I would encourage you to read my book on manhood, *God's Gift to Women: Discovering the Lost Greatness of Masculinity*.[2]

The importance of this area is grossly understated even in our Christian community today. A marriage, a wife, and a houseful of children can't help but thrive when the man of the home is thriving spiritually.

Food for Thought (If You're Not on the Same Spiritual Page . . .). Sometimes it takes time for both partners to adopt a unified spiritual passion and direction. If you have started your marriage without being on the same spiritual page, then take some time to gain a clear vision for this area of your life together. Discuss what your goals and desires are for spiritual growth. When it comes to church and denominational issues, it's important to talk about your feelings and expectations, then coordinate your church direction *together*. Going to the "perfect" church is not as important as growing together spiritually. In fact, the most significant spiritual growth in one's life usually takes place in personal times of study and worship—not in a church building. Church is not meant to be the fuel for your spiritual fire—your individual relationship with Christ is what will keep your spiritual flame burning. So don't become so focused on making church decisions that you lose sight of what *really* matters—your passionate daily walk with your King, both personally and as a couple. If you focus on keeping Christ in His proper place in your lives and marriage, you will naturally begin to grow together spiritually.

- Leslie -

Step #2: Tackle Responsibilities Together

The first ninety days of marriage are the ideal time to come up with a plan for tackling all of life's many responsibilities. It's easy to assume that your husband will handle the finances or that your wife will do all the cooking, but those assumptions can lead to resentment and daily friction in marriage if not discussed ahead of time. If you and your spouse can learn to work *together* to conquer the daily tasks of life, then you will experience a level of success and fulfillment most modern couples only dream of. You will be ten times more effective as a team than if you try to tackle life separately. Take some time to sit down as a couple and talk through each area of your day-to-day life as a couple. Decide which areas each of you will be in charge of individually and which areas you will handle together. For example, maybe your husband will oversee the majority of the finances, but you will sit down together each week to pay bills. Maybe your wife will manage basic household chores, but you both will devote every Saturday morning to thoroughly cleaning the house as a team. If you take time *now* to agree on who will do what, years of frustration and friction will be avoided.

Keep in mind that in order to thrive as a team, you might have to surrender your preconceived ideas of what areas your spouse is to be in charge of. Once upon a time, a "good wife" meant one who spent all day cooking, sewing, and scrubbing floorboards; and a "good husband" meant one who was up at 5:00 a.m., plowing the fields and chopping firewood until dusk. But that model doesn't always work in today's modern world. It's true that God desires men and women to take on certain roles in marriage. As discussed earlier, He created man to take the spiritual leadership and "head" position in a home. But being a spiritual leader doesn't mean a husband isn't capable of washing dishes or doing laundry. Far from it! In fact, the best leaders are those who are willing to serve selflessly—doing the tasks that no one else desires to do.

God created women to oversee and manage their homes, to love their husbands and children and make them the top priority. But that doesn't mean a woman can't also run a business, be active in ministry, or manage financial investments. (Just read about the incredible wife, mother, and successful business-woman in Proverbs 31.) Of course, being a woman who is successful in business or ministry doesn't mean that same woman should be above mopping the floor. Neither spouse should try to prove that he or she is above menial tasks. Rather, each spouse must focus on serving each other and working together toward a common goal. Remember that God is far more concerned about each spouse loving and serving the other like Christ than about who scrubs the toilet and who pays the bills.

As you sit down to discuss the various areas of daily life, be sure that you aren't taking unnecessary assumptions into the conversation. Guys, if your mother always picked up your dirty laundry and had three hot meals on the table every day, that doesn't mean your wife needs to follow in her footsteps. Girls, if your dad spent every weekend repairing the roof or staining the deck, that doesn't mean your husband must do the same. Remember that you are starting a *new* family unit—and your individual responsibilities need to be tailor-made to fit your unique life together.

Rather than focusing on the "traditional responsibilities" of which spouse manages household tasks, finances, etc., it is far more practical to approach each area in light of your personal life situation. Which of you has more time to devote to certain responsibilities? Which areas are each of you more inclined toward? Household chores and daily tasks aren't usually much fun, but we all have certain things we don't mind doing as much as others. Work on dividing up life's tasks according to the time and personal preferences that each of you have. Be willing to make compromises along the way to serve your spouse. For example, Eric can't stand doing laundry, and I can't stand cleaning bathrooms—so we have agreed that every weekend he will do one while I do the other. Ask yourselves how you can practically divide life's tasks *equally* so that you both have time for rest and relaxation, not to mention time for cultivating your marriage relationship and your walk with God.

Food for Thought: Learning Basic Life Skills. For many modern couples starting out in life, basic skills must be learned in order to effectively manage a home. Growing up, not many of us are taught how to keep a budget, change a tire, or even wash a load of white towels without inadvertently staining them pink. And we take that lack of training into our marriages. Unfortunately, this can lead to serious problems—both in life effectiveness and in our marriage relationships. If one spouse does all the housework simply because the other one doesn't know how to start the washing machine or turn on the vacuum cleaner, this is a sure recipe for tension down the road. If your finances are a mess because one or both of you have no idea how to maintain a budget, this sets you up for unnecessary marital stress as the months and years pass.

Don't become impatient or frustrated just because you are skilled in a certain area in which your spouse is not. Simply take time to patiently help him or her learn. If *both* of you struggle with certain areas—like cooking or managing finances—then consider getting outside help. Do you have a friend or a relative who is great at managing finances? Ask for his or her advice. Or find a basic financial management course and attend it together. Do you know someone who is an excellent cook? Invite him or her over to show you the foundational skills of putting meals together. There has never been a better time for you to become excellent in basic life skills than right now—at the very start of your life together, before sloppy habits begin to be formed.

Banish Laziness. Laziness is a common issue that plagues modern marriages. "My husband just sits on the couch every night while I cook and clean the kitchen," a new bride moaned to me recently. "My wife never helps me with projects around the house—she just gives me a 'honey-do list' and expects me to take care of everything," I heard one of Eric's football buddies complain the other day. Sometimes what is perceived as laziness is merely a lack of communication. Your husband may not realize you would like him to help with the meals. Your wife may not understand that you need her assistance with repair jobs around the house. As you take time to talk through each daily life task, be sure to express your expectations and desires to your spouse. Sitting down now and asking your spouse to be involved in a certain task is far more effective than nagging, pouting, or punishing him or her later.

Laziness can also be attributed to plain old exhaustion. The fast pace of our modern lives sometimes causes us to spend all of our energy on things outside the home. At the end of the day, we often have no energy left to spend on household chores. So when you and your spouse discuss how to handle household chores, be sure that you designate times during the week when you know you will have energy to accomplish the tasks. (For instance, Eric and I prefer doing them first thing in the morning or on weekends.) If you and your spouse structure your life together in a way that allows for rest and relaxation as well as getting necessary tasks accomplished, then you will avoid the common complaint of laziness that is often just a result of poor planning.

Of course, sometimes laziness stems from nothing but pure selfishness. Marriage presents constant opportunities to lay down our own selfish agendas and take on Christ's attitude—selflessly serving our spouses. If you find yourself lounging on the couch when you know your spouse would appreciate your help with something, take that opportunity to yield to Christ's agenda rather than your own. Getting up off your comfortable sofa may not feel good at first, but the rewards you will reap in your marriage relationship will be well worth the sacrifice.

The same goes for purposely doing a poor job in a certain area in order to get out of doing something you don't want to do. Men often get a bad rap as the ones who intentionally mess up household tasks so that their wives will get frustrated and take over—freeing the men of that particular responsibility. Eric has never enjoyed cooking on charcoal grills—or cleaning them afterward, for that matter. During the first year of our marriage, he would constantly "forget" how to operate our archaic charcoal grill, thus cutting down on the number of times I asked him to cook on it. But soon I realized that there was a reason he kept forgetting—he simply didn't want to retain the information! The reality was that he hated that grill—in fact, he also conveniently "forgot" to pack it in the moving van when we moved from Michigan to Colorado the following year!

But men aren't the only ones with selective memories. Women can play the game as well. When Eric and I were first married, I hated doing the dishes because we didn't have a garbage disposal—a luxury I had been used to in the past. I couldn't stand scraping the leftover food off the plates and into the trash. Often I would "forget" to scrape the food off the plates, causing the drain in the sink to clog. Eric hated having the drain clogged with soggy food, so doing the dishes quickly became an area that he took charge of. But the real reason I "forgot" to scrape the plates was because I wanted Eric to do all the work.

As you work through the different areas of life responsibility, allow God to show you any areas of laziness or selfishness. If there is an area that you are particularly bad at, make sure you have not purposely sabotaged your skills in order to get out of doing it. Tackling life's responsibilities shouldn't be a competition to see who can get out of doing what, but rather a *team effort* in which both of you are working toward a common goal.

As a couple, take some time to talk through the following areas and develop a unified vision for how you can tackle them as a team.

Finances

- Which spouse will be in charge of paying the bills, or will you pay them together? When, during each week or month, will you take care of paying the bills?

- Will you have separate or joint bank accounts? What about credit cards?

- Will you have a monthly budget? Who will be in charge of balancing your checkbook and maintaining your budget records? Will you do it together? If so, how often?

- How will you make decisions regarding major purchases? Since finances can be a major cause of marital conflict, it is wise to come up with a "code of conduct" for making financial decisions as a team.

Food for Thought: Staying on the Same Financial Page. Eric and I agreed early in our marriage not to spend significant amounts of money on anything unless we were both in agreement—even if we had to pass up "great opportunities" because we couldn't talk it over first. This principle has saved us from making many hasty and foolish decisions. For many couples, getting on the same financial page is as simple as sitting down and having a discussion about your priorities and deciding together when and how you are going to pay for that next car, piece of furniture, or vacation. But some couples have financial priorities that don't seem to mesh. The husband might be more interested in paying off the house than he is in having furniture in the living room, while the wife might feel that life is on hold until the house is furnished and decorated. The husband might want to spend extra money on a new car, while the wife would rather use the money to pay off student loans. If you find that you and your spouse are clashing in the area of financial priorities, consider the following action steps:

1. Take some time to pray about the financial decision individually, and allow God to show you if you are holding on to your own agenda for selfish reasons. Are you thinking of the money as *yours* or as something that belongs to both of you? (And by the way, it doesn't matter which of you goes to work to earn the money. You are in covenant with your spouse—and everything you have belongs to both of you.) Are you willing to make compromises and sacrifice some of your own plans in order to preserve marital unity? Ask God to help you see the issue from your spouse's vantage point and not just your own. And ask Him to help you serve your

spouse while also being responsible with the money He has entrusted to you.

For example, Eric feels more secure and responsible when we are saving our extra money rather than spending it. But there are times when he knows that he can best serve me and our marriage by laying down his desire to have excess cash in the bank. When our son was born, we were faced with extreme challenges that caused us not to get more than an hour or two of sleep at one time, throughout the day and night. After four months of this, I was at a physical and emotional breaking point. I told Eric that I needed help, and he listened. We chose to use money in our savings to hire an overnight nanny for a month so that both of us—especially me—could finally get some sleep and recover from the most exhausting season we'd ever experienced. It wasn't easy for Eric to spend our extra money this way, but he did it as an act of selfless love for me, and it meant the world to our marriage.

Sit down with your spouse and discuss the possibility of a compromise—a way in which both of you can feel that your financial priorities are being honored. For instance, maybe you can continue to pay off the house, but at a reduced level so that you can also buy living room furniture. And maybe you don't have to buy the most expensive living room furniture but can settle for something middle-of-the-road to keep some money free for paying off the house. Maybe you can take a vacation closer to home and spend less on the trip so that you can also get that new lawn mower you need.

2. Come up with a clear rule of thumb for handling debt. Discuss how you feel about debt. What kinds of debt, if any, do you feel comfortable taking on? Are there any kinds of debt that you *don't* feel okay about? Many couples we know have decided that a mortgage and a car payment are acceptable, but they don't want to be enslaved to credit card debt. Debt can be a major stress on a marriage, so you are wise to carefully think through this area in the beginning of your life together. Setting guidelines for how you want to handle debt it will help clarify your financial decisions and priorities, and you can keep each other accountable to sticking with the plan.

3. If you and your spouse are already carrying large debts that are out of control, are having trouble staying within a budget, or simply can't agree on financial priorities, then consider seeking the help of a professional financial counselor. Getting an outside perspective can help you see the bigger picture and may go a long way in helping you reach a point of agreement and begin working toward a common financial goal. If you do choose to get outside help, be sure you work with someone who isn't trying to "sell" you something and who has a biblical perspective on finances. Check with your local church for resources, or visit some Christian Web sites such as www.family.org (type "money" into the search feature) or www.crown.org to get started.

Household Chores

1. Who will handle the cleaning of your house, or will you do it as a team? When during the week/month will you take care of the cleaning? Are there certain jobs that you each will take on? For example, every Saturday morning Eric and I set aside three hours to deal with household maintenance. He cleans the bathrooms and mows the lawn; I clean the kitchen, vacuum, and do laundry. This way, we each have specific jobs to accomplish and we don't waste time arguing about who is going to do what. Tackling the cleaning as a team helps us get the tasks done quickly so that we can enjoy the weekend, and we avoid frustration with each other because we are both working together. Take some time to adopt a unified game plan for cleaning that fits your time and lifestyle.

2. Who will handle the grocery shopping and cooking? Will you take turns? Will you do it together? Are there certain meals of the day when you will "fend for yourselves" and others when you will sit down to eat together? It's also important to discuss food preferences. If one spouse will be doing the majority of the cooking, take some time to find out what your spouse does and doesn't like to eat rather than making assumptions. Try to plan meals that factor in both of your tastes. For a season of our marriage, I was a vegetarian while Eric ate meat. I didn't want to force him to eat according to my tastes or special needs, so I made meals that could be made

with *or* without meat. There is no reason that one spouse has to be miserable while the other enjoys his or her food preferences. Be creative in coming up with meals that work for both of you—even if you have separate dishes from time to time.

3. How will you handle other shopping needs, such as clothes and gifts? Will you shop together? How often? How much money will you allot for these items?

4. Talk through all the other responsibilities that apply to your home, things like repairing the fence, feeding the dog, planting flowers, mowing the lawn, changing lightbulbs, etc. Discuss which of you will take care of each area, and how often you plan to do it. Remember to be as equitable as possible in dividing up chores. Your goal is not to try to dump as much as you can on your spouse, but to work together to accomplish the tasks so that you have time for more important things—like spending time together.

5. Once you have discussed your plan for handling tasks and household responsibilities, you may find it helpful to write the plan down and put it in a place where you can easily refer to it. Eric and I found it helpful to keep a chart, on which we would write down each task, the responsible person's name, and how often it needed to be done. Every month or two, we would refer back to our chart to see how well things were working. Eventually, taking care of household

tasks and life responsibilities will become so habitual that you won't need to have anything written down. But in the beginning, it can be a very helpful tool in gaining momentum as you begin the daunting job of running a home. Also, be open to tweaking your plan according to changing life circumstances. Don't force your spouse to keep doing certain jobs just because he or she originally committed to them. If your spouse discovers that he or she simply doesn't have time to accomplish everything, be willing to pick up the slack without complaining.

Children. Most couples don't have to make major decisions about raising children in the first ninety days of marriage, but this is such a big area that it is wise to begin talking about it ahead of time. You may have already discussed when you want to have kids or how many you'd like to have (though if you haven't, now is a good time!), but it's important to think through this subject at a deeper level. When and if you do have children, will one spouse be the primary caregiver, or will you share the load? How do you feel about having child-care help, such as babysitters or day care? What kind of schooling do you want your children to have (public school, Christian school, home school)? Even though you may change your thoughts on these areas once you actually *meet* your future children, it never hurts to be as much on the same page with your spouse as you can ahead of time.

The first year Eric and I were married, we spent hours talking about how we wanted to raise our future family. We had a wonderful time dreaming about the future together. We gained a unique vision for how we wanted our parenting experience to look one day. And even though it was quite a few years later that our first child was born, we remembered and implemented many of the thoughts and ideas we had discussed during our first year together as husband and wife. We started our parenting journey as a unified team, because our vision for parenting was formed at the beginning of our marriage.

Note: If you *do* have children going into marriage, then you aren't adjusting to life as just husband and wife, but also as parents in a new family situation. Take some time to get on the same page about how you want to raise your children as a team from this point forward. If you are finding the transition difficult, it might be very helpful to get some input from a pastor or biblical counselor.

Step #3: Leaving and Cleaving—Becoming Your Own Family Unit

God said that a man shall "leave father and mother, and shall cleave to his wife" (Matthew 19:5 KJV). In the first ninety days of marriage, you are doing more than just learning how to love and serve each other; you are forming a whole new family unit. No longer are you merely "Bob's son" or "Karen's daughter." Now you are *Mr. and Mrs.* Both of your names are on the marriage license, and your lives together have launched a whole new family into existence.

During the beginning of your husband-and-wife relationship, learning to "leave and cleave" is absolutely vital to the long-term health of your marriage. New habits must be formed. In the areas where you have always leaned on your parents, now you must learn to lean on your spouse instead. In areas where you sought to please your parents, now you must first and foremost please your spouse. If you have been independent of your parents prior to marriage, leaving and cleaving still must be learned. Instead of making your own decisions and taking care of yourself, you now must learn how to make decisions *with* your spouse and learn how to take care of each other. Where you shared your deepest thoughts and feelings with your close friends, now you must learn to share them first and foremost with your spouse. This is not to say that you must cut off the relationship with your family members or stop sharing things with your close friends. But it is vital that you learn to make your spouse your primary depository for sharing your feelings, fears, hopes, and dreams. Leaving and cleaving means that your spouse—not your parents or friends—now has primary access to the depths of who you are.

Leaving and cleaving can seem more like a vague theory than a tangible task. But if you are purposeful about developing new habits in the beginning of your life together, you can make great strides toward solidifying your marriage into a new family unit. Here are some ways to make it happen.

Protect Your Spouse's Trust. You should be the person your spouse trusts most deeply above all others. You—above anyone else—should hear the deepest thoughts, fears, and dreams of your spouse's heart. But your husband can't share freely with one he can't trust implicitly. Your wife can't open her soul to one who doesn't hold it sacred. So make a commitment to each other in the very beginning of your life together that you will protect each other's trust. Prove to your spouse that you are a safe depository. If your husband confides in you his fears, he must have the confidence that you won't divulge that information to your friends. If your wife tells you her personal struggles, she must know that you won't repeat that information to your family members. If you are unsure where to draw the line between what is appropriate to share with others and what is not, then it's best to err on the side of caution. Unless your spouse specifically gives you permission to share something personal with others, it is safer to assume that you should keep the information private.

When you protect each other's trust, you set the stage for becoming lifelong best friends. Eric is my best friend in the world, and I am his. I tell him things that I would never tell anyone else, and I know that he will honor my secrets. He confides in me, and he never questions whether I will repeat his words to others. We have implicit trust between us, and therefore, we can share the depths of who we are—without fear.

Go to Your Spouse for Advice. It's easy to default to old habits—especially when it comes to asking for advice from others. Maybe your parents have always been your sounding board. Maybe you have a mentor or a best friend who always helps you gain a clearer perspective on your life. But now that you are married, your spouse should become your new primary consultant for all of life's perplexities. While it can still be healthy at times to gain outside input and exhortation, it is usually best to do so as a couple. When confusing circumstances hit, let your spouse be the first person you go to. Ask for her input. Ask for his thoughts. And take your spouse's advice seriously. Even if you need advice in an area you don't think your spouse knows much about—such as finances or career decisions—your spouse has special insight into your life. He or she observes you more closely than anyone else. So listen to what your spouse has to say.

Whenever we are going through a time of confusion, Eric and I like to steal away to a coffee shop and talk. Eric is a great sounding board for me as I try to gain a big-picture view of my life and where I am headed. And when Eric needs to wrap his mind around a foggy set of circumstances, I help talk him through the process. Going to your spouse first protects the unity of your marriage and strengthens the foundation of your new family.

A Note to Men on Giving Advice: When women have a problem, often they don't need a problem solver as much as an empathetic listener. Guys are natural Mr. Fix-Its. Solving problems is one of a man's specialties. But be aware that your wife may simply want you to validate her emotions and understand her concerns. Before you step into problem-solving mode, take a few moments to simply listen to what your wife is saying. Show genuine interest in how she is feeling. Ask questions. Repeat back what she is saying—in your own words—to let her know you have heard and understood. Only after she feels that she has been heard should you ask her if she wants your help in seeking a solution. And when you do problem-solve, make sure that you don't criticize or correct her, but tenderly exhort her to be everything Christ wants her to be.

A Note to Women on Giving Advice: Your husband must feel respected if he is going to be comfortable seeking your advice. It might be tempting to point out all of the ways in which your husband could have handled the situation better or to draw attention to his blind spots. Resist the urge to criticize or nitpick. Instead, honor your husband by noticing the positive things he contributed to the situation. Point out the good qualities that he has, and don't dwell on the bad ones. Let him know that you admire him and believe in him, and you will be amazed at how his confidence increases. When your husband senses that you are his cheerleader rather than his disapproving critic, he will gain the strength to overcome bigger and bigger challenges with each year that passes.

Be Loyal to Your Spouse. Often your friends and/or extended family will have expectations for how you should spend your time or resources. But as you form a new family unit with your spouse, those expectations should not dictate your decisions. Now you must have a new protocol for making decisions—considering your spouse above all others. Of course, it is still important to be sensitive to your friends' and family's desires. But it is even more important to be considerate of your spouse's needs and desires.

Guys, if you must choose between what your buddy wants and what your wife wants, put your wife first. Girls, if you must choose between what your mom wants and what your husband wants, put your husband first. Does your mom expect you to call her every day, at the expense of time with your husband? Put your husband first. Does your buddy expect you to spend every Saturday afternoon with him instead of your wife? Put your wife first. If your husband doesn't want to spend every holiday with your parents, then don't force him to just because you are still trying to please Mom and Dad. If your wife is uncomfortable around certain friends or family members in your life, don't force her to spend excess time with them simply because *you* enjoy their company.

When it comes to making the daily decisions of life, your loyalty should be first and foremost to your spouse. Obviously there are some exceptions to this rule: If your spouse is asking you to do something un-Christlike, you shouldn't agree to it— even for the sake of loyalty. And there are certainly plenty of ways to maintain sensitivity to your friends and family members and still be loyal to your spouse. But if it ever comes down to a choice between serving your spouse and pleasing other people—serve your spouse. Prove with your life that you are loyal to your spouse above anyone else on this earth, and you will demonstrate leaving and cleaving at its best.

Step #4: Making Decisions Together

As a single person, you were used to a certain level of independence. When it came to making decisions, you called the shots. If you wanted to stay out late on a Friday night, that was your prerogative. If you wanted to change careers, that was your choice. And if you wanted to spend all your money on a set of bagpipes, it was your money to spend. Now that you are in covenant with your spouse, you have exchanged your independence for something different—*interdependence*.

That Olympic figure-skating pair mentioned earlier cannot hope to win the gold unless they depend on each other. They must make their twists and turns in sync with each other. If one goes in his own direction, not only does the beauty of their presentation crumble, but serious injury can result. The same is true for marriage. Unless you and your spouse learn the art of interdependence, you will risk serious damage to your relationship. It is not honoring to your marriage if you come home from work one day and announce to your spouse that you took a promotion and you both will be moving to another state. It is not respectful of your spouse to decide to spend all your spare time pursuing your PhD without first consulting him or her.

Yes, learning how to operate as a team is initially more work than rushing ahead with your own agenda. But in the long run, your marriage will function far more effectively if you practice interdependence—working in sync with each other like that polished figure-skating pair.

Here are some practical ways to approach decision making as a team:

Don't Rush the Process. Taking that job in Tallahassee or buying that red convertible might seem an incredible opportunity in the moment. But if you take time to evaluate your decisions and discuss them together, you will be saved from many foolish, spontaneous actions. And you will have the added confidence that comes from knowing the decisions you do make have been carefully thought through. It's best to think through a decision when you aren't in the heat of emotion. The age-old advice to "sleep on it" is actually good common sense. Let the idea settle for a day or two before you begin to seriously evaluate it. Then take some time to clear your schedule and spend some focused time discussing the decision with your spouse. Don't try to make major decisions with the television on or the phone ringing. Go to a place where you know you won't be interrupted. Spend as long as you need talking through the details of the decision. Share your perspective on the situation, but also take time to really stop and listen to your spouse's perspective as well.

And if you haven't come to a place of agreement after your discussion, decide that you will give it a little more time and then revisit the situation. Decisions made when one spouse is not truly supportive can cause major conflict in your marriage relationship. So make an effort to get as close to being on the same page as possible before you take a step forward in any direction. If, after your discussion, you both feel that an outside perspective would be helpful, then set up a time to talk through the decision as a couple with someone you respect and trust. Even then, don't allow that person's advice to be your sole decision-making criterion. You and your spouse are the ones who receive the benefits or reap the consequences of the path you choose to take.

Consider Your Spouse Above Yourself. It's easy to evaluate a decision from only your perspective. You may be thrilled about a job promotion that will move you across the country. But take time to consider how the change will affect your spouse. Will he or she be pulled away from a hard-earned career, an important ministry, or close relationships? Try to see the situation through your spouse's eyes. If you put your spouse above yourself, your marriage will thrive, even if your career doesn't. If making a certain decision will benefit you but greatly challenge or inconvenience your spouse, then be willing to sacrifice your desires in order to put your spouse first. That doesn't mean your spouse may not eventually agree to go in the direction you desire. But let it be your spouse's willing choice—not just a reluctant agreement to your choice. Prove with your life and attitude that your spouse is far more important to you than any job, opportunity, or material possession you could ever pursue.

Get God's Perspective. When it comes to decision making, it is vital to yield to Christ's agenda rather than forge ahead with your own plans. Be sure to take time to seek God's direction, both individually and together. Carve out significant time in your schedule (more than just five minutes) to quiet your mind, pray, and allow God to gently reveal His perspective to you. Just as it is important that you allow God to expose any selfish agenda you have in regard to your finances (as mentioned earlier), it is vital to do the same when it comes to other major life decisions. We so often make decisions based on our own desires. We want to pursue things that will secure our comfort and happiness. But God is not primarily concerned with our comfort and happiness. He is concerned with our hearts. And sometimes He asks us to walk the more difficult road in order to mold us even more into His likeness. Don't base your decisions merely on what *you* want. Surrender to His lead. Allow Him to shape your desires rather than following the trends of the culture around you. In the long run, God's plans for you are far more fulfilling than your own.

When we are faced with a tough decision, Eric and I often take time individually to pray and wait on God. We write down any insights we feel God is showing us about the issue at hand. Then we get together and share those things with each other. We also spend time praying together as a couple, asking for God's lead. For extra-important decisions, we spend a few days fasting and praying diligently about the situation. God doesn't always make our path crystal clear. But we take time to seek Him and put Him first. And then we make the best decisions we know how to make, trusting that He will open the right doors and close the wrong ones as we move forward. There are many times when we feel we are shooting in the dark when making a decision, but as we build our lives around Christ, He never lets us down.

Keep in mind that you should never use your relationship with God to manipulate your spouse. It is not appropriate for you to announce to your spouse, "God told me we should move to Cincinnati, so pack your bags." God doesn't work that way in a marriage. His desire is to build unity, not discord, between you and your spouse. Sure, it is possible that He may nudge you in a direction that your spouse doesn't necessarily see as the best. But that doesn't mean you should start calling all the shots whether your spouse likes it or not. Give your spouse time to gain God's perspective. Pray that God would show your spouse the same things He has shown you. And trust that He is more than capable of changing your spouse's heart in His own time and way. Dominating, controlling, or manipulating your spouse won't help you fulfill God's purpose for your life. God is far more interested in seeing you yield to Him than in what job you choose or where you decide to live. When it comes to decision making, focus first and foremost on surrendering to Him and honoring your spouse, and He will take care of the rest.

Step #5: Explore Each Other's Unique Life Purposes

The first ninety days of marriage are the perfect time to study your spouse at a deeper level, to begin to really understand what makes him or her tick. Don't just assume that you already know your spouse. Your spouse's heart and mind are an endless frontier to be discovered. If you treat marriage as a daily opportunity to learn more and more about your spouse, you will be amazed at the depth of friendship and intimacy you can find.

Take some time to sit down with your spouse and explore each other's unique gifts, desires, passions, and purposes. Eric and I have found that asking each other certain questions has greatly assisted us as we've explored each other's unique gifts and passions. You can use the questions at the end of this section to get started, and add more of your own if you desire. Be sure to choose a time when you will not be interrupted. It shouldn't be just a five-minute conversation. In fact, you may need to have several different discussions in order to really delve into your spouse's life purpose and desires. It might be a good idea to choose one discussion in which you ask your spouse these questions, and a different discussion in which your spouse asks *you* the questions. Like Eric and me, you may find it beneficial to take time to individually write down your answers to these questions and then exchange them with your spouse. That way, you can be sure you have time to really think through your answers instead of just speaking off the top of your head.

When You Are Asking . . . As you listen to your spouse's passions, desires, and dreams, focus on really hearing what he or she is saying. Ask specific questions to help draw out the deepest thoughts and desires of your spouse's heart. A few years ago, Eric asked me what ministry opportunities I desired to pursue. I told him I was excited to continue and expand my work with young women. Instead of just nodding and saying, "That's great," he probed deeper. He asked questions about how I hoped to see my vision realized. What kind of young women did I want to work with? What was the message I felt compelled to share with them? How, specifically, did I want to go about reaching these young women? Write a book? Start a magazine? Develop a Web site? Disciple one-on-one?

Because Eric was willing to take the time to explore the desires of my heart, he actually helped me articulate and shape one of my greatest passions. Eric wasn't just a passive bystander in the conversation—he got personally involved in helping shape my vision. He became excited about the possibilities. He encouraged me to pursue my desires and reminded me of the ways that God had equipped me to pursue those desires. By the end of the conversation, I had more than just a general desire to work with young women; I had a clear and specific vision and purpose for this area of my life.

Your attitude toward your spouse's dreams will build either confidence or insecurity in his or her life. Many a spouse has been massively stymied because of the negative words of his or her marriage partner. Remember that God has given you the privilege of being your spouse's cheerleader. You are the one who can help your spouse reach his or her full potential. So take your position seriously. Don't just show mild regard for your spouse's interests and pursuits. Get involved. Help your spouse shape his or her desires into a clearer life direction and vision. Encourage your spouse in the areas he or she is gifted in. Give your spouse the confidence to pursue the things he or she is passionate about. Become your spouse's biggest fan. You will be amazed at how your spouse will come alive when you do.

When You Are Answering . . . As you answer the following questions, be as specific as possible. You may not feel you have much clarity about where your life is headed, or even about the dreams and passions of your heart. If that is the case, take some time to prayerfully let God begin to awaken you to new possibilities. Think about the things in life that have made you feel most alive. Have you enjoyed taking care of young children? Do you feel strangely drawn to serve people in a foreign country? Are you fascinated with history or literature? And as you begin to recognize your desires, allow God to gently shape them. Even if your dreams seem foggy at first, through time, prayer, and talking with your spouse, God will bring them more and more into clear focus. Start with what you know now, and allow this to become an ongoing exploration that you experience with your marriage partner. Even after eleven years of marriage, Eric and I love to ask each other these questions. Each time, we learn new things about each other and delve even deeper into the endless frontier of each other's souls.

Questions to Ask Your Spouse

- For what, specifically, do you sense that you are here on earth?

- What specific message do you think God has given you to share with the world?

- If you were going to share that message, how would you want to share it?

- At what moments in life do you feel most alive?

- At what moments in life do you feel closest to me (your spouse)?

- At what moments in life do you feel closest to God?

- What issues in life do you feel most strongly about?

- If you had to pick a "cause" to fight for, what would your cause be?

- What one thing could I do (as your spouse) to best assist you in being all that God has called you to be?

- What do you feel are your strongest attributes? What do you feel are your greatest weaknesses?

- What dreams do you have in life? What do you dream of doing a year from now? Five years from now? Ten years from now? Fifty years from now?

- If you could take one aspect of our marriage and make it incredible, which aspect would you choose?
- At the end of your life, what do you want people to say about you?

In a Nutshell

Marriage is about a man and a wife becoming the ultimate team. It's not about just the wife serving her husband or just the husband serving his wife; it's about both of them serving each other simultaneously. It's about a prince and a princess treating each other as true nobility and more important than themselves.

As the prince of the home, the husband holds the privileged position of being the champion of his wife's future. Far too many men today limit the potential of their wives. They mentally fence in a woman's potential impact and subconsciously assume that a godly woman can be nothing more than a wife and a mother. A great husband learns to catch *God's* vision for his wife's life. A Christ-built husband seeks to empower and enable his wife the very way Christ seeks to empower and enable His bride. He becomes a champion for her life, studying her, cheering her on, helping shape her into a world-impacting princess.

As the princess of the home, the wife has heavenly eyes for her man. She believes in him, she applauds his hard work, and she is his biggest fan in the world. To be a great husband, a man desperately needs a great wife. His strength and confidence hinge upon her admiration and emotional support. The more of Christ a wife shows to her husband on a daily basis, the more his impact will be upon the world each and every day. A princess of the home is both a gentle breeze and a mighty rock in her husband's life. She provides refreshment, encouragement, and tenderness when her husband is weary from life's battles. And instead of nagging or manipulating when things are difficult, she offers exhortation and inspiration to motivate her man toward greatness.

A great team is one in which each member is constantly watchful of the other's needs and eager to help meet them. The members of a great team make decisions together and never independently of each other. A great team *shares* the weighty responsibilities of life. A great team, if built well, can carry a marriage through the harshest struggles, the most extreme crises, and the hottest trials.

Chapter Five

HOW TO BUILD THE ULTIMATE ROMANTIC SANCTUARY

True romance is not a thoughtful act, but a thoughtful lifestyle. True romance is a state of mind, an attitude toward life, a way of living.

- Eric -

It's far too easy to let marriage romance slip away. The wonder of being newlyweds can create some extraordinary romantic moments in the weeks and months following the Big Day. But once the new-car smell begins to fade in the relationship, romance often takes a backseat to the cares of life. If you haven't noticed, our culture isn't built to foster romance in marriage. Instead, it's designed to foster extreme selfishness and extreme degrees of stress. And it just so happens that there are no more effective saboteurs of romance than selfishness and stress. As modern couples in search of happily ever after, we have to be intentional about how we choose to live out our marriages in this romantically challenged culture.

Romance isn't cultivated in the midst of harried schedules, cluttered houses, and microwave dinners eaten hastily in front of *Seinfeld* reruns. Romance doesn't thrive with exhausted husbands sacked out in the lounge chair in front of the nightly news and haggard wives chasing screaming kids around the house.

For romance to thrive, there is need for more than roses, rhymes, and sentimental rhetoric. There is no harm in a husband's offering a daffodil to his distraught wife as she runs out the door, shouting, "Thanks, dear! I'll see you tonight at ten after I pick Junior up from hockey practice!" But to label it "romance" is a bit generous. Like great sex, true romance is not a thoughtful act, but a thoughtful lifestyle. True romance is a state of mind, an attitude toward life, a way of living. True romance isn't the giving of a daffodil, but the entire structuring of a life around order, beauty, simplicity, and serenity. True romance is a life full of daffodils.

The Principle of Sanctuary

Somehow we have been taught that stress and chaos are just part of life. But Leslie and I strongly believe that God does not want us to accept the modern workaholic, stressed-out, out-of-control lifestyle as required punishment for being human. In fact, we believe that God is a huge fan of order, beauty, simplicity, and serenity. We have certainly realized that stress and chaos are easy to find and integrate into life. But we have also discovered the invigorating and liberating feeling of building a marriage and a home around God's principle of sanctuary.

God's principle of sanctuary is simple: *protect and preserve that which is most important.*

Leslie and I have spent quite a few composite months of our marriage praying about and discussing what we feel is most important in our lives. It's actually surprising how many things in our lives can claim massive amounts of time but yield paltry results. For instance, football. I love watching football, playing football, and reading about football in the paper. But really, how is football enhancing my life and my relationships? Why should we waste our time pouring ourselves into activities that mean nothing to our lives and provide only a spark of temporary satisfaction? Why not spend ourselves on the things that really matter? That is what the principle of sanctuary is all about.

When we determine what really matters in our married lives, it is then important to build our lives around those few sacred things. Four years ago Leslie and I made some radical changes in our lives in order to protect the things that really mattered. At that time we were traveling around the world speaking about romance and relationships. We had a full schedule, and we were rarely at home. But strangely, even though we were talking seemingly twenty-four hours a day about romance, we had begun to lose the romantic life we had always taken for granted. Airports, security check-ins, airplanes, rental cars, hotel rooms, living out of a suitcase, and late-night meals at the Waffle House—these were not proving to be prescriptions for an ever-growing romantic existence. We found that our time for each other was eroding, and our time for God was being trumped each day with urgent matters. We didn't have a lifestyle that allowed us to smell daffodils or watch sunsets. We were driven, always producing, never just living.

So we decided to radically alter our life together to ensure that our relationships with God and with each other were paramount. We gave up speaking, and at the risk of our entire ministry platform, we decided to build a simple life around the enjoyment of God and the enjoyment of our family in the small town of Windsor, Colorado.

It was the principle of sanctuary at work. And while the principle of sanctuary does produce extraordinary and enchanting results, it also inevitably comes with a price. By halting our speaking career, we were removing ourselves from the public eye, and in the book and music business, that can be a noose around your career's neck. In modern ministry, it is workaholism that gets you noticed, that creates opportunities, and that proves to the world you are popular and worth listening to. Choosing a quiet existence in a small town was a ticket to anonymity, not stardom. Our decision to protect the things that really mattered came with a cost.

It's one thing to talk about the principle of sanctuary, but it's quite another to prove it with the practical side of your life. Yes, our ministry was forever altered by our decision.

Now we have a ministry built on the principle of sanctuary, and, strangely, it is far more effective. But, more importantly, we rediscovered order, beauty, simplicity, and serenity. Whatever the cost, sanctuary is worth it. And I speak from personal experience when I say this: "It's better to have the bread of the simple and serene than to have the rich banquet of the stressed-out" (Proverbs 15:17, author's paraphrase).

As a couple, you have a choice in how you will live out your married life together. Either you can have a lifestyle that reflects heaven's beauty, or you can have a lifestyle that showcases this world's crazed frenzy. It's our prayer that you will use these first ninety days of your marriage to begin to implement the principle of sanctuary in your life. Don't wait until the romance has evaporated and your relationship is on the rocks before you recognize what really matters. Romance grows like a million daffodils in the soil of sanctuary, and as long as sanctuary is maintained, those daffodils will continue to grow more and more fragrant and beautiful throughout your life together.

Marriage Enchantment

I like to live life as if I have a background movie score playing. When I'm standing in front of a hostile crowd, I picture a deep bass movie-trailer voice saying, "Eric Ludy was just one young man, standing courageously against the odds. They mocked him! They ridiculed him! But in the end . . . he inspired them!"

It's all part of the romance. Remove the movie score and the narrator's deep bass voice, and you have just a miserable situation. Life will throw a thousand curveballs our way, but put the right movie score behind each and every challenging scene, and suddenly the story transforms from depressing documentary into romantic drama.

Marriage is supposed to be the stuff of cinematic wonder, not a dull science-fair production on the reproductive habits of squid. Kendall, a bride of ten months, recently described her marriage to me this way: "We come home from work every night, sit on the couch, and eat leftovers in front of the TV, then crash into bed at ten. It's the same routine every single day." Too many of us accept the dull, dismal, disillusioned nature of life as normal and fail to fight for the mystical romantic glow. Marriage has the potential to be the most extraordinary journey into the heart of heaven itself, but finding that lifelong luster takes a bit of childlike imagination and trust and a whole lot of hard work.

God designed marriage to be enchanting. I really like the word *enchanting*. It's a word tailor-made for fairy tales and storybook endings. Whenever I hear it, I think of a secret mountain alcove dressed with a million wildflowers all wafting in a summer breeze. The word *enchanting* is used to describe something that captivates, fascinates, and enthralls.

As hard as it may be for some to believe, God actually designed marriage to be enchanting—a lifelong discovery of ever-deepening affection, a captivating journey into the heart

of another, a fascinating exploration up the mountain of intimate love, and an enthralling love story that plays out like a
God-scripted screenplay. God designed marriage to be a life
of amazing love with a background movie score attached.

The word *enchanting* also invokes a sense of mystery and
mystique. Enchanting things aren't found dancing in public
squares and twirling on top of really tall buildings. Fairy tales
have taught us that enchantment is found only in faraway
places—places difficult to reach, out of the way, and usually
guarded by large monsters and magical spells. Enchanting
things are hidden things, private things, preserved things.
To those of us who have read fables and fairy tales, it is intu-
itive that enchanting things are never found in the bustle of
busy society, but in the quiet solitude of the meadowland, where
the simple beauties of God's creation have been preserved.

Falling in line with all the fairy-tale adventures of love and
romance throughout the ages, an enchanting, captivating,
fascinating, and enthralling marriage is discovered in the very
same way. When the sacred sanctuary of married love is preserved, marriage blossoms in intimacy and never stops growing in its beauty.

The enchantment of marriage is found by those who know
how to preserve the sacred meadowlands of their lives. The
marriages of those who never lose the secret mountain alcoves
will always be captivating. Those marriage partners who never
allow the glory of simple sunsets to lose their roseate luster will
never cease to find fascination and delight in intimate love.

Those who know how to protect and preserve that which matters most in marriage will bathe in the glories of lifelong romance.

Speckled across our nation are many parks and wildlife preserves—large chunks of the most gorgeous land cordoned off to be forever free of developers, hunters, and graffiti artists. These lands are vigilantly protected, carefully monitored, and diligently kept free of all that would taint or compromise their beauty. Every great marriage must learn this very same secret of sacred set-apart space.

In the first ninety days of your new life together, it's important to take the "most gorgeous" portions of your life and cordon them off as national parks. As a couple, make for yourself a private sanctuary—a place that you vigilantly protect, carefully monitor, and diligently keep free from all that would taint or compromise its beauty.

A Lesson in Marriage Real Estate

So how do you take portions of your life and cordon them off as protected places? Marriage is obviously not a plot of land. But marriage is made up of sacred, enchanting elements that must be protected and preserved. And like land, a marriage has elements that can be considered public and others that must be considered private. There is "real estate" within a marriage that is perfectly fine to open up to the world about, and there is sacred territory upon which a No Trespassing sign should hang. The captivating, fascinating, and enthralling nature of marriage depends on a couple's healthy understanding of marriage sanctuary.

Each marriage possesses some extraordinary plots of land. These exquisite plots of land are God's wedding gift to you as a couple. Some of this land is for you as a couple to share with friends and family in your life. But the most "gorgeous" property is meant to be cordoned off and turned into a private preserve. Far too many couples today don't comprehend the value of these precious meadowlands laden with enchantment. Immediately following the honeymoon, these lovers pronounce the amazingly lush alcoves of sacred intimacy to be public lands and subsequently invite any and all to come and visit, set up camp, and pick wildflowers.

"Dude, you wouldn't believe what Julie did last night!" I overheard a husband say, sharing with his buddy the details of an intimate marriage moment.

"Matt finally opened up and told me why he's been so moody lately," a bubbly bride said to her friend, then proceeded to spill all the details of the sacred conversation.

When these properties are invaded by every Joe Schmo this side of the Mississippi, they quickly lose their value and their inherent beauty. For the sake of an ever-growing intimacy in your marriage, make these intimate areas part of your personal marriage preserve.

Start with the Bedroom

Honing the art of sanctuary takes some work. A bit of practice is necessary to figure out how to make sure your life is full of daffodils. I can promise it will take longer than ninety days to master this all-important art, but it's important to get started right at the beginning of your marriage.

The best place to start practicing this valuable art is in your own bedroom. A couple's bedroom is the perfect training ground for sanctuary excellence. Since a couple's bedroom is the location for the most intimate and sacred activities of a marriage, it's also a great place to start protecting and preserving all that is truly important to a couple.

Make your bedroom a private preserve. Guard it, keep it clean, keep it beautiful, and make it a place that you as a couple love to be. Treat it as a set-apart place, an alcove of enchantment, a place untouched by the outside world, reserved just for the private enjoyment of you and your spouse.

To Leslie and me, our bedroom is our getaway. It is always clean, fresh, and private. Our bedroom is designed for romance; it is built as a place we love to be. It is our private retreat where the mysteries of our very personal romance unfold. No one other than us knows what takes place inside that room. And as a result, the secret activities that play out there are both magical and heavenly.

When you learn to keep *your* bedroom sacred for your marriage, the romantic benefits of this effort will quickly become apparent to you both. You will find that it's not just your bedroom, but your entire home that must become a sanctuary. Your bedroom is the sanctuary for your marriage, while your house is the sanctuary for your family. The mystery only continues to unfold and blossom within your heart and mind when you realize that your very body is meant to be a sanctuary for the God of the universe.

The art of sanctuary consists of two very important elements:

1. Sacred time
2. Sacred space

A bedroom is the perfect place in which to start blending these two beautiful elements. A bedroom can be far more than mere square footage in your house; it can become "sacred space," an enchanting alcove overrun with the romantic fragrance of a million daffodils, in which "sacred time" can be spent cherishing and adoring your spouse. Shut the door, lock the door, and ensure that the wildflowers are available only for you and your spouse to pick.

Sacred Time. Leslie and I share almost every sleeping and waking moment of life. Since we work at home together during the day, we have an extremely unusual situation that allows for lots and lots of shared time. But only a small amount of this time is sacred time. When we are sleeping next to each other at night, it's nice, but it's not sacred. When we are eating breakfast together in the morning, it's great, but it's not sacred. And even when we write books together about romance and relationships, it's inspiring, but it's not sacred time spent together.

Being around Leslie during the everyday normal stuff of life is not sacred time; it's ordinary time. Ordinary time can be delightful, but sacred time is enchanted. Sacred time is of a completely different nature than ordinary time. It's focused time specifically designed to adore and cherish a spouse. It's private, it's guarded, and it's intentional. Life's cares and concerns are not allowed inside sacred time. Fascinating news about the next-door neighbor's successful gallbladder surgery is not allowed inside sacred time. Even writing this paragraph about sacred time in marriage is not allowed inside sacred time. Sacred time is . . . well . . . sacred.

Leslie and I love sacred time. It's our time to cherish each other, to enjoy each other, and to express to each other our appreciation and adoration. Some of our most beautiful memories are found curled up in the tender arms of a sacred moment together.

We usually take a walk before our sacred time to make sure we've both been able to get all the business details out of our minds so that when our sacred time commences, we both will be fully present. We've found that the concerns of life can easily sabotage our sacred time. As you likely have found in attempting to have quiet alone time with God, it's easy to be distracted in sacred time.

In these first ninety days of marriage, don't just focus on having sacred time, but focus on figuring out what attempts to sabotage your sacred time. Whether it's stress, mental distractions, busyness, disorder, or the unromantic nature of smelly underwear draped over the back of a chair—figure out what hinders your sacred time as a couple, and then do whatever it takes to remove that element from your sanctuary. (We will discuss this concept in greater detail in the Putting It into Action section of this chapter.)

Every Saturday when Leslie and I schedule the details of our upcoming week, one of the most important things on our to-do list is sacred time. We make it a priority. And sacred time goes beyond merely scheduling a date night once a week. Sacred time is something we attempt to plan for and cherish each and every day of the week. To us, marriage is our daily romancing of each other.

Sacred Space. As a couple, treat your bedroom as sacred space. Don't decorate your bedroom with friends and family in mind. Decorate your bedroom as if it will never be seen by anyone besides you and your spouse. Treat it as a private haven, a secret alcove of intimate beauty. Just because it is a room in your house and you have the door closed does not make your bedroom sacred space. For the area of your bedroom to be truly a cherished, sacred space, three things must be true about it:

1. It must be completely private.

2. It must be clean and fresh smelling.

3. It must be a desirable place to be.

A sacred space doesn't have to be dressed up with plush fabrics or decorated with expensive artwork to be a sanctuary of heavenly romance. It just needs to be protected and preserved. Throughout your marriage, your sacred space should be tended like an ever-beautifying garden. With the passage of time, it can certainly become more fragrant and more fanciful, but it is important to note that what makes it a desirable place to be should never be the decor, but the *lover* who awaits you there.

The Discipline of Sanctuary

When your life is disciplined around the things of life that really matter, you are the happiest of people.

The word *discipline* makes quite a number of people squirm. "Legalism!" some claim. "Misery!" others howl. "I'm incapable!" still others insist. But every human is capable of discipline. And no, discipline is neither legalism nor misery. It's freedom! Discipline is simply spending the energies of life on the things that matter most. Discipline is ensuring that nothing robs your time and attention from the things that truly give you life. Discipline is not easy, but neither is it misery. When your life is disciplined around the things of life that really matter, you are the happiest of people.

Protecting the sacred time and the sacred space in your life takes discipline. As a couple, you must become trained soldiers standing guard at the entry points to these priceless lands. Boundaries must be set in place to preserve the most important things in your married life. These boundaries must be guarded and daily maintained. All distractions and hindrances to a healthy marriage must be eliminated. This takes watchfulness and an amazing amount of focused effort. Every word that you speak in public about your private life as a couple must be guarded and carefully monitored. A sanctuary can be discovered only by a couple who take marriage intimacy seriously.

In living with a spouse, you can have merely a house in which you both reside, or you can create a marriage sanctuary in which your romance blossoms. You can have merely a bedroom in which you sleep, or you can have sacred space in which the smell of a million daffodils is in the air. You can have a lifestyle of chaos, stress, and the pursuit of money and fame, or you can have a life that exudes the order, beauty, simplicity, and serenity of heaven.

For Leslie and me, marriage is one of life's purest and most perfect delights. But marriage becomes a cherished element of life only when it is guarded and tended. If you choose now— in these first ninety days—to build your lifestyle and home into a sacred sanctuary for your love, we promise that you will discover a depth of fulfillment few couples today ever find. And you will also find that as the years pass, your marriage will only become more and more spectacular.

Here's to a lifetime of secret sacred moments together!

Putting It into Action

- Leslie -

Step #1: Bring Your Priorities into Focus

Force yourselves to be ruthless in protecting the things that matter.

As you just read, the purpose of a marriage sanctuary is to protect what is most important. Instead of allowing anything and everything the world offers to worm its way into your new life together, it is vital to identify the things you value the most and then work together to jealously guard those things. Before you can begin building a sanctuary around your highest priorities, you must first bring your priorities into focus so you have a clear idea of *what* you are working to protect.

Define Your Priorities. Take some time to clarify the things that matter most to you. Individually, write down a list of your top five to ten priorities, in order of their importance to you. Then exchange lists with your spouse. Discuss which of your priorities are similar or different. Decide together which priorities matter most to you as a couple. What are the things you most want to serve and protect in your new life together? When you have defined the areas that are most important to both of you, create a joint list of your top priorities. Eric and I have defined our top priorities in life in this order:

1. *Serving God.* Cultivating and protecting the intimate relationship we share with Him.

2. *Serving each other.* Meeting the spiritual, emotional, and physical needs of each other.

3. *Nurturing our son.* Meeting his spiritual, emotional, and physical needs.

4. *Serving our extended family (both biological and spiritual).* Cultivating and protecting the relationships that God has strategically placed in our lives.

5. *Serving the needy and the lost.* Delivering the truth of the gospel to those in need, with both our words and our actions.

Keep your priority list in a place where you can see it often and be reminded of the things you value most as the weeks, months, and years go by. Whenever life takes a hectic or stressful turn, Eric and I remind each other what our true priorities are, and they help clear away the fog and keep us headed toward the right destination as a couple.

Step #2: Create Healthy Boundaries

It is one thing to define your priorities on paper, but it's far more challenging to actually build your life around those things—to vigilantly serve and protect the things that matter most. Your true priorities aren't just the things that are written on paper; they are the things you guard and protect, the things in which you invest the majority of your time and energy. Many of us *say* our highest priority is our relationship with God, yet we spend the largest portion of the day watching TV or pursuing our careers. We might *want* our relationships with our spouses to be at the top of our importance lists, but if we spend far more time surfing the Internet or talking on the phone than we do building intimacy with our spouses, we have nothing more than good intentions for our marriage relationships. It is not enough to want the right priorities. We must orient our *entire lives* around the right priorities.

A sanctuary cannot exist in the middle of a busy interstate. A sanctuary is a set-apart place, with protective walls around it to keep out noises and distractions. To build your home into a marriage sanctuary, you must build healthy boundaries into your life to protect the things that matter.

As the saying goes, saying yes to one thing means saying no to something else. Boundaries help us say yes to things that reflect our highest priorities and no to the things that don't.

Examine Your Daily Life. Take some time to think through how you spend your time during a typical day. What claims the largest part of your focus and attention? Individually, write down answers to the following question:

Approximately how many minutes/hours each day do you spend on each of the following activities?

Sleeping   _____

Eating   _____

Working   _____

Being with God   _____

Talking with your spouse   _____

Being with friends/family   _____

Watching TV   _____

Sitting at the computer   _____

Talking on the phone   _____

Doing housework   _____

Doing hobbies   _____

Doing other activities   _____

Once you have answered the above questions, compare this list with your list of top priorities. As a couple, take some time to talk through the following questions:

1. Are you each spending your time and energy on your true priorities?

2. Are there distractions that are claiming more of your focus and time than they should?

Define Your Boundaries. Prayerfully consider some practical steps you can take—both individually and as a team—to guard your true priorities in life. For example, if watching TV is hindering your time to build your relationship as a couple, write that down as a priority threat. If sleeping late in the morning is causing you to miss spending time with God, write that down as something that needs to change.

Force yourselves to be ruthless in protecting the things that matter. It might sound painful to give up your two hours of Internet time each night or that extra forty-five minutes of hitting the snooze button each morning, but keep in mind what you will be gaining as a result—a life full of zest and forward movement, a marriage in which you thrive as a team, and a purposeful, peaceful existence that most people only dream about in today's world. If you want the best that marriage has to offer, you must become like an athlete in training. Remember that you are aiming for an Olympic gold medal, not fourth place in the three-legged race at a church social.

Creating healthy boundaries is most effective when it is done early in your life together as a couple. Put the right things in their proper places, before the wrong things have a chance to sneak in and stake claim over your priorities. From the first year we were married, Eric and I have carried quite a bit on our plate—book deadlines, speaking tours, recording projects, endless ministry tasks, and most recently a new baby to raise. Early on, we realized that we needed to set boundaries in our life together to protect the things that mattered. We have seen too many Christian marriages fall apart from lack of healthy boundaries—couples who failed to guard their relationships with God and each other. So we don't take our boundaries lightly—they are the foundation stones that make our life together work. Every year, we modify our boundaries slightly to adapt to new seasons of life. But here are some of the basic safeguards that protect our marriage sanctuary:

1. We set aside our mornings for time with God and each other. We start our day with joint prayer, we carve out time individually for Bible study and growing in our walk with God, we eat breakfast together (where we talk together instead of reading the newspaper), and as often as possible we take a long walk together before we start our workday. In order to protect our mornings, we ban the snooze button, the phone, the TV, the Internet, and work projects during this part of our day.

2. We spend most of our leisure time together. Though Eric loves to watch football games, he intentionally chooses not to spend his Sunday afternoons and Monday nights screaming at the television. I enjoy shopping. But rarely do I spend my time that way. Instead, we choose to spend our free time focused on building a deeper relationship with each other—going on picnics together, reading a good book next to the fire, or visiting a local coffee shop for a cup of chai and a philosophical chat. Sure, Eric watches an occasional Broncos game, and I spend a day at the mall every once in a while—but only when we have agreed together to spend some time apart doing things we enjoy individually. We make sure we are spending the majority of our down-time growing closer together as a couple. Yes, it is a sacrifice for us to give up things we enjoy individually. But the sparkle we gain in our relationship as a result makes the effort well worth it.

3. We end our workday at a specific time, and we don't discuss ministry, finances, or any other work-related topics at night. We typically don't even answer the phone after our workday ends; instead, we let voice mail take messages and we return calls the next day. We don't spend time on our computers at night. We don't spend our nights in front of the TV. Instead, we use our evenings to be together as a family: to eat dinner together, sit on our front porch and talk, or—our newest activity—take our baby son to the park. Putting boundaries around our work and ministry tasks is one of the most challenging things we've done to protect our marriage sanctuary. Since we are both type A people who love productivity, working too much is one of our biggest weaknesses. But though our work is important, our marriage is much higher on our priority list. Keeping our work in check and our evenings protected gives our marriage the time and focus it deserves.

Following are our suggestions for steps you and your spouse might take to set up boundaries in your life together: **As a couple, agree on the boundaries you want to implement in order to protect your marriage sanctuary, and write them down.** The boundaries that you set in place to protect your marriage sanctuary might be different from ours. You might need to cut down on outside social activities, reduce the time you spend on hobbies, or reorganize your work schedule so that you and your spouse have quality time together each day. The important thing is to identify all the things in your life that could steal your time and energy from your true priorities—and then ruthlessly create boundaries for each of those things.

Along with each boundary, write down any practical steps you must take in order to make the boundary work. For example, if you decide to put boundaries around your work time, write down the specific time you will commit to being home each day.

Keep your list of boundaries in a place where you can refer to it often, and make sure you follow through on the practical steps necessary to put your boundaries in place. Don't put it off. The sooner you implement your boundaries, the sooner you will discover the amazing benefits of a marriage sanctuary. Your boundaries may feel uncomfortable at first, but as they become a habitual part of your life, you will begin to appreciate how they protect and enhance the things that matter most.

Food for Thought: Doing Whatever It Takes. Keep in mind that as you examine your daily life and priorities, you may recognize something in your life that needs to be *completely eliminated* rather than just "trimmed back." If you or your spouse has a job that causes you to feel that you never see each other, be willing to consider a career change. If either of you has a friendship or a hobby that is undermining your marriage relationship, be willing to cut it out of your life.

As discussed earlier in this chapter, Eric and I have had to make radical changes in order to protect the principle of sanctuary in our life together. When we were considering ending our eight-year stint of full-time touring and speaking, many people advised against it. "There is so much need out there," some argued. "How can you just turn your back on people who need your message?" Others told us, "You are shooting your ministry in the foot by choosing to stop traveling." But God was whispering a different message to our hearts. He was calling us to protect the most precious foundation stones in our marriage, reminding us that true ministry could flow only from a life built around eternal things.

Though it was certainly not easy, ending our touring lifestyle was one of the best decisions we ever made. Our marriage and our walk with God began to thrive again. Peace and fulfillment replaced stress and exhaustion. Our sanctuary came to life once more. When you are willing to take radical steps to protect things of eternal value, you will find that the rewards are more than worth it.

Keep Your Marriage Private. Just as it is important to set boundaries around your time and activities, it is so vital to adopt a "code of conduct" for how you speak about your marriage. As discussed earlier in this chapter, boundaries must be established around what you share with outsiders. At the beginning of your new life together, your marriage is like wet clay. If you allow the outside world (including your family) to put their fingers all over the clay in this stage, it won't set properly—your clay will be imprinted with everyone else's marks instead of your own. So decide together that you will keep your marriage private. Discipline yourselves not to let friends or family members in on all the details of your new life together. They don't need to know about your sex life, your first argument, or the irritation you feel when your spouse forgets to put down the toilet seat. Sharing meaningless marital information with others, such as what you had for dinner last night or where you are planning to go for vacation, is harmless. But for the most part, it's best to keep the details of your marriage relationship sacred—something that only the two of you share.

Girls, it can be tempting to call your mother or best friend after a fight with your husband and share all the intimate details. But it is far more honoring to your husband to keep your mouth shut. Your mom or best friend doesn't need to hear about the insensitive things your husband said—in fact, if she does, it will most likely only tempt her to take third-party offense against your husband. Consider writing in your journal instead—process your emotions with Christ rather than letting a friend or family member gain access to a private area of your marriage relationship. If you feel that there is a serious issue in your marriage for which you need outside input, consider talking with a pastoral couple or a professional biblical counselor.

Guys, it can be tempting to joke with your buddies about your wife's annoying habits or brag about your hot honeymoon escapades. But it is far more honoring to your wife to keep those things private. She will be able to open her heart to you far more fully if she knows that you won't expose her weaknesses or intimate secrets to the world. Telling friends and family about an argument or intimate moment is like inviting them into your home to stand there and observe your private life together. To truly become your own family unit, you must protect the privacy of your marriage.

In my first few months of marriage to Eric, there were two areas that seemed to be an endless source of curiosity to outsiders—finances and children. We were constantly being asked details about our income situation and our plans for having children. So we decided that we would not discuss our personal finances or plans for starting a family with other people, other than in general terms. Every time someone asked, "So when are you two going to have kids?" we would just smile and say, "You'll have to wait and see." Whenever someone casually queried about our finances, we would shrug and say something vague, such as "God meets all our needs." And if someone really pressed the issue, we would tell them that it was an area we had decided not to discuss with others. We have maintained these guidelines throughout our life together, and they have given us a sense of privacy that has greatly benefited our marriage relationship.

Think through the areas that you need to keep sacred in *your* marriage, from finances to personal conversations, to decisions about having children. Write them down and then stick to your decision—no matter how tempting it may be to share juicy details with outsiders. As you protect the private areas of your marriage, you will experience the incredible fulfillment of knowing that you are your own family unit—leaving other relationships and cleaving to each other.

Step #3: Set Proactive Goals

Knowing your priorities and keeping them protected are the first two crucial steps in creating your sanctuary. Now, it's time to *cultivate* the areas of your life that matter most. A sanctuary is like a private garden—the soil must be tilled, the plants must be watered, and the flowers must be pruned in order to keep the environment beautiful. To experience a beautiful marriage and a passionate walk with God, it's not enough to simply carve out time for those relationships—they must be *nurtured* in order to grow healthy and strong.

Define Your Specific Goals. Look at each of the priorities on your list, and take some time to set proactive goals for each of them—both individual goals and goals you share as a couple. To grow in your relationship with God, your proactive goals might look like these:

Individually:

- Set aside one hour each morning for prayer, Bible study, and journaling.

- Choose a book of the Bible to study, and purchase the study tools needed (e.g., study guide, concordance, commentaries, etc.).

As a Couple:

- Select a historical Christian biography (see the recommended reading list on our Web site, www.whenGodwrites.com, for ideas) to read together. Set aside a half hour each evening to read it aloud and discuss it together.

To cultivate your marriage, your proactive goals might be:

Individually:

- Do one special thing for each other every day (e.g., a little love note, some words of encouragement, unsolicited help with a project, etc.).

As a Couple:

- Spend at least one hour every day getting to know each other better (e.g., asking each other questions about different areas of life, finding out tidbits from each other's childhoods, listening to each other's dreams and desires for the future, etc.).

- Set aside a day or evening each week to be together, and plan a romantic activity ahead of time (e.g., cook a romantic candlelit dinner together, map out a scenic hike and picnic, etc.).

Food for Thought: Keeping a Running List. You can make a similar list for each area of your life that you feel is a top priority. Eric and I keep a running list of our current goals for each priority in our married life. Every two months or so, we sit down and revisit our list of goals and see how we are doing in keeping them. If we find that we have allowed life to become too busy to stay up with our goals, we discuss changes we can make in our lives in order to allow more time for us to focus on them. Or, if we are going through an unusual season of life (such as in the months after our son was born), we simplify our goals to be more realistic, instead of just giving up on them. Keep your list of goals in a place where you can refer to them often—daily if possible. And be sure to plan a time every month or two to sit down together and evaluate how you are doing in being proactive with your priorities. Be aware that it might take some time before it becomes natural to build these goals effectively into your life. If you find you are not doing well in keeping your goals, don't give up on them. Instead, reorganize your life and/or simplify your goals until you find a rhythm that works.

Remember that just because you are working toward specific goals in these areas doesn't mean you can't enjoy spontaneous times of talking with God or unplanned special moments with your spouse. Quite the opposite. The purpose of goals is to help you cultivate the most important relationships even in the busyness of everyday life. As those relationships grow strong, spontaneous moments that enhance your relationship with God, your spouse, and your family will be a natural result.

Step #4: Create a Healthy Home Environment

One of the most important aspects of a marriage sanctuary is the *physical environment* in which you cultivate your romance with each other and your relationship with God. It's hard to have an effective prayer time with the TV blaring. It's difficult to share a night of beautiful intimacy with your spouse in a room that smells like dirty laundry. The first ninety days of marriage is the best time to build a home environment together in which your sanctuary can truly flourish. Whether you live in a one-room apartment or a five-story mansion, whether you are a neat freak or consider yourself cleaning-impaired, whether you have money to spare or only have a spare eighty-three cents a week, you can create a home environment in which your marriage sanctuary will thrive.

Any environment can become a sanctuary. I was greatly inspired by the story of Corrie and Betsy ten Boom—two courageous women thrown into a Nazi prison for harboring Jews in their home. Betsy had always had a gift for making things beautiful—for making a house into a haven. But could a prison cell be made into a haven? Corrie described walking past Betsy's cell and getting a glimpse of the sanctuary that had somehow been created there. "Unbelievably, against all logic, the cell was charming," Corrie wrote. "The straw pallets were rolled instead of piled in a heap, standing like little pillars among the walls, each with a lady's hat atop it. A headscarf had somehow been hung on the wall. The contents of several food packages were arranged on a small shelf. Even the coats hanging on their hooks were part of the welcome of that room, each sleeve draped over the shoulder of the coat next to it like a row of dancing children."[1]

As you work to build your home into a marriage sanctuary, remember that you don't need a huge house or a wad of money to make it happen. You just need to work creatively with what you *do* have. The attitude in your home is far more important than the material things in your home. If you focus on creating a haven for your marriage, four simple walls and a ceiling can easily be turned into a beautiful palace.

Gain a Vision for Your Home. Contrary to popular belief, creating the right home atmosphere is not just for people who have a knack for decorating or love hanging out at Home Depot. And it isn't supposed to be an area that one spouse (often the wife) takes charge of while the other (often the husband) "tunes out." Sure, one of you might be more involved than the other in certain aspects of building your home. But it is crucial that you and your spouse pursue a shared vision and purpose for your home environment and work together to see that vision become a reality. Even if one of you has already been living in your house prior to your wedding day, it is still important to start fresh in creating an environment that reflects your new life together as a couple. (Guys, your grungy bachelor pad look might not work anymore. Or ladies, your girly decor might have to go.)

Your home is the setting in which your marriage sanctuary will be built. Most of the significant moments in your relationship with God and your relationship with each other will occur within the walls of your house, so this area of your life is worthy of some focus and attention. Use the following questions and suggestions to help get your discussion going:

1. What type of atmosphere do you want your home to exude? Eric and I desire our home atmosphere to be *peaceful, creative, organized,* and *fun.* Describe *your* ideal home atmosphere in three or four words.

2. What factors will contribute to this atmosphere? Some factors that contribute to the atmosphere of our home are an uncluttered environment, well-organized living and work areas, creative photos and artwork on the walls, and music that we enjoy. Make a list of things that could (or currently do) help you achieve *your* desired home atmosphere.

3. What factors will detract from this atmosphere? The factors that can easily detract from our peaceful atmosphere are

TV, unrestricted phone calls, and messy, disorganized rooms. Make a list of factors that could (or currently do) detract from *your* desired home atmosphere.

4. How will other people (family, friends, neighbors) fit into your home environment? Do you want an "open-door" policy, where people are welcome to show up at any time unexpectedly? Or do you want your home to be a private retreat, where people come over only when invited? Eric grew up in an "open-door" home, and I grew up in a "private-retreat" home. There were benefits to both environments. Both were hospitable and warm, but those traits were expressed in completely different ways. Eric and I realized that we needed to agree on how we would handle this area as a couple. Because of our public, people-intensive ministry, we decided that a "private-retreat" home atmosphere and form of hospitality would best protect our sanctuary.

Decide which approach, "open door" or "private retreat," best fits *your* lifestyle and priorities. You may decide on a blend of the two. You both may need to make sacrifices in order to come to a unified vision in this area. The purpose of your home environment isn't to serve your own selfish wants, but to cultivate your marriage sanctuary. So do whatever it takes to put your sanctuary first. If you have a friend who always hangs around your house and robs you of your time together, no matter how much you like your friend, the time he or she spends in your home must be curbed.

5. Gain a vision for your quiet-time area. Eric and I each have a place in our house where we go to cultivate our relationship with God. We make sure there are no distractions in that area of the house (like the phone or a pile of unfinished work). We have agreed on when each of us will spend our individual times with God, and we don't interrupt each other during those quiet times. We have our journals, Bibles, and study materials easily accessible in our "quiet-time spots." We have worship music available to listen to in that part of the house. The environment we create for our quiet times makes a world of difference in our ability to cultivate our relationship with God.

What kind of atmosphere do you feel will best cultivate your own quiet times (e.g., worship music, uninterrupted quiet, etc.)? Individually, write down a list of things that could (or currently do) help you each cultivate a healthy quiet-time environment. Then write down any practical steps you must take in order to build that kind of atmosphere (e.g., organize your study materials in that area of the house, purchase a journal and store it in your quiet-time spot, have worship music ready to play, etc.).

What kind of things will detract from your individual quiet times (e.g., TV, phone, reminders of work projects, interruptions from your spouse, etc.)? Individually, write down a list of things that could (or currently do) cause distraction in your quiet times. Then write down any practical steps you must take to remove those distractions (e.g., unplug the phone, remove the TV, keep reading materials—such as newspapers and magazines—in a different part of the house, etc.).

6. Gain a vision for your bedroom. As discussed earlier, even though you are building your entire home into a marriage sanctuary, it is important to have a special place, like the bedroom, that is tailor-made specifically for your intimate time as a couple. It is all too easy to allow the bedroom to become just another room in your house, letting televisions, computers, phones, or piles of work find their way onto your bedside table. But for intimacy to thrive, an intimate atmosphere must be created and protected. The bedroom is the most sacred part of a marriage sanctuary, the place in which your intimacy will be nurtured. Eric and I decided early in our marriage not to allow phones, computers, television, or work projects into our bedroom. We even agreed to make certain topics of discussion off-limits in our bedroom, such as finances and work deadlines, because we noticed how much those conversations put a damper on our intimate time together. Identifying and removing intimacy hindrances is a vital first step in creating a set-apart place in which to cultivate your romantic relationship.

Remember, intimacy isn't hindered only by things like televisions and computers. Dirty clothes strewn on the floor, a stack of mail piled on the dresser, or the subtle smell of Fido (your beloved unwashed pet camped out on your bedspread) can easily kill a romantic experience. Write down any distractions that could (or currently do) distract from the intimate atmosphere of your bedroom.

Next, take some time to discuss specific ways in which you can turn your bedroom into a haven for cultivating intimacy. Eric and I create an intimate atmosphere with fresh flowers, candlelight, and romantic music. What special things could contribute to *your* intimate times together?

Step #5: Build Your Home Environment

Once you have gained a clear vision for the kind of home environment you desire, it's time to begin building that environment. If, after answering the questions above, you feel that your home environment is already exactly the way it should be, then you probably don't need to read this particular section. But if you are like most couples, there are many practical things that must be done in order to build the right atmosphere for your marriage sanctuary. Creating a healthy home environment does require some effort. But by taking time now to make your home a marriage sanctuary, you set the stage for a lifetime of "happily ever after" by creating the cottage or castle in which your fairy tale can come to life.

Creating Systems. When you were single, maybe you were in the habit of tossing your dirty socks on the floor and leaving them there. But now that you have chosen to share your home with another, you have given up your right to leave your socks wherever you please. Your sanctuary is a place that you must build and maintain together. It is important to *agree* on where you are going to leave your socks from this point forward. This may seem an insignificant decision. But more than a few marriages have been severely affected by a pair of dirty socks lying on the bedroom floor!

This is where systems come in. Systems create an ongoing plan for dealing with dirty socks and piles of mail. It isn't enough to simply acknowledge that a stack of mail in your bedroom is a detractor from an intimate evening; you must remove the pile of mail and implement a plan to make sure tomorrow's mail doesn't end up in the same place. Your home can become a marriage sanctuary only when all those little areas of life are carefully and purposefully dealt with.

Some say that being organized as a couple is a matter of preference or personality rather than necessity. And certainly that is true to a point. To have a healthy marriage sanctuary, you don't have to alphabetize your credit cards or color-code your closet. But taking time to create some basic systems for your new life together will help safeguard your home environment and protect your marriage sanctuary. Systems prevent arguments over dirty socks, annoyances over piles of junk mail, and hundreds of other little irritations that can build up over the months into major marital issues. Systems protect your home atmosphere against all the little things—from television to junk mail—that can subtly creep in and destroy your sanctuary. So whether you enjoy getting organized or not, remember that the time you spend creating systems is an invaluable investment in your marriage relationship.

Following are some of the most important areas in a modern home environment for which systems must be created. Take time to read through each area and personalize the suggestions to your own situation. If you already have a successful system in place for that area, feel free to skip over it. And if you think of additional systems you need to create for your own specific lifestyle, be sure to write them down and discuss them.

The Phone

Handling Phone Calls. If you and your spouse have plenty of uninterrupted time to focus on your relationship, then you might not need to create a plan for handling phone time. But if you are like most couples, you need focused time each day to connect with each other and spend time together without interruption from the outside world. Start by determining if there is any time of the day when you will purposely ignore the phone (such as during dinner or during your evening hours together). If you think that hearing the phone ring will compel you to answer it even during the off-limit times, you might need to implement a plan for turning off the ringer or keeping the phone in a different room (the same goes for cell phones). Write down the time(s) of day you have agreed not to take phone calls. And if necessary, write down a plan for taking messages and returning calls. Do you need to get an answering machine or voice mail? Do you need to get caller ID so you can answer only the urgent calls? Write down any action steps you need to take to make your phone plan work.

The Computer

For many modern marriages, the computer causes more conflict than all the other "household issues" combined. Internet surfing, e-mail, instant-messaging, and computer games are just some of the seemingly harmless activities that can quickly strip away your valuable time together and undermine your marriage sanctuary. And then there are the incredible dangers of Internet pornography—poised and ready to entice you with every trip into cyberspace. So if you choose to have a computer and access to the Internet, don't underestimate the significance of creating a careful plan for this area of your life.

Handling Computer Activities. Now that you are sharing your life with another person, you are accountable to your spouse for the way you spend your time and the activities you choose to do—including computer activities. When you were single, maybe you spent many a Sunday afternoon playing computer games or instant-messaging your friends. Now that you are married, your computer habits may need to change. It is important that you decide *together* what computer activities you will allow into your home. As a couple, discuss what role the computer will play in your home. Will you use it only for e-mail? Will you use it for shopping, and if so, for what kinds of things? Will you use it for playing computer games, browsing certain Web sites, visiting certain discussion forums, visiting chat rooms, or instant-messaging? Talk about the specific computer activities you feel are appropriate for your home and marriage sanctuary. Write down the specific role the computer will play in your home. Defining what your computer is there for will help keep it in its proper place.

Handling Computer Time. Time spent on the computer can quickly get out of control. You sit down to check your e-mail or visit your favorite sites, and what you intended to take five minutes suddenly turns into two hours. So it is wise to come up with a plan for making sure the computer doesn't rob you of time to be spent on your true priorities. As a couple, discuss how much computer time you feel is appropriate for your marriage. Is there any time of day when it would be wise to make the computer off-limits? Do you need to implement a system for helping keep your computer time in check? For instance, do you need to set the alarm on your watch when you sit down at the computer so that you don't end up spending more time there than you intended? Do you need your spouse to help keep you accountable to stay within your allotted time frame? Should you keep your computer in a remote part of the house so you aren't tempted to use up all of your free time in front of the monitor? Write down any action steps you must take in order to implement your computer time plan.

Guarding Against Internet Dangers. Internet pornography has claimed a prominent place in cyberspace. If you aren't proactive about protecting yourself from Internet porn, it can quickly find its way onto your computer with one careless click of the mouse. The makers of porn sites are relentless in their attempts to lure you at every opportunity. One moment you might be shopping online for space heaters, and the next moment an offensive message flashes in front of you. One minute you might be checking your e-mail, and the next you are bombarded with offensive photos. Internet pornography is typically far more addictive and dangerous than any other form of its kind, since it can be viewed in private, without the shame of having to procure a magazine or video. Allowing any form of this slime into your mind and home environment will immediately destroy the sacredness of your marriage sanctuary. But there are several things you can do to protect against this marriage enemy. Be proactive in putting the right barriers in place. Here are some starting points:

- **A Plan for Pop-up Porn and Offensive Spam.** There are many resources on the Internet to help you deal with the ever-changing threats of spam and pop-up tactics. You can find programs that control Web page content by doing an Internet search such as "Internet content filter." You can also search "How can I stop getting spam?" for additional information. And many Internet service providers offer "family controls" that filter out adult content. Check with your Internet provider about which of these services they offer, and shop around until you find one that meets your needs. You can also check www.spamabuse.net.

- **A Plan for Guarding Against Internet Pornography.** You can find helpful information on protecting your home from Internet pornography on Web sites such as www.family.org and www.nationalcoalition.org. There is also a service called Covenant Eyes that is designed specifically to keep computer users accountable for the material they look at online. Eric and I use the Covenant Eyes service. At the end of each month, a list of all the Internet material we viewed individually during the past month is sent to each other's e-mail addresses. It's a great system. Find out more by visiting www.covenanteyes.org.

As a couple, discuss and write down your plan for guarding against offensive material and Internet porn and any action steps you must take in order to implement this plan.

Your Stuff

Sharing a home with another can take some getting used to. As a single person, you had the freedom to throw a pile of clothes on your bed and leave them there for a week. If you wanted to keep your bike helmet in the middle of your bathroom floor, you could. But now decisions about where to put your dirty socks, your furniture, and your prized childhood collection of model airplanes must be made *together*. You will avoid endless hours of conflict if you simply take time to agree on systems for dealing with all the "stuff" of life. Following are some of the most common areas that need to be discussed when learning to share a home with your spouse. As you go through this list, feel free to add other areas to your discussion if needed.

Clothes/Laundry. Where are you going to keep your clothes? Will you share a closet? If so, which side will be yours, and which side will be your spouse's? Will you each have certain drawers in the dresser in which to keep your clothes? If so, which ones? Do you have a designated area for dirty clothes? These may seem like basic questions to address, but having a system for clothes storage can help you avoid many of those proverbial fights over closet space and laundry hampers. If you don't communicate about what to do with dirty socks, your spouse may never realize that throwing them on the bedroom floor annoys you. If you don't create a system for sharing closet space, you can end up hogging all the hangers without knowing it. Write down your plan for where to keep clothes and laundry, along with any action steps necessary to implement this system.

Bathroom. If you don't have the luxury of having two separate bathrooms, it's important to discuss a system for where you will keep your bathroom "stuff." Will you leave your toothpaste and shaving cream sitting out on the counter? If not, where are you going to keep them? Will you each have separate drawers or cabinets for your individual bathroom stuff? If so, which ones? And believe it or not, it's even important to discuss that age-old marital issue—the toilet seat. If you have strong feelings about putting it down after use, communicate your desires to your spouse. Be willing to change your habits in order to keep harmony in your marriage sanctuary. Write down your plan for your bathroom stuff as well as any action steps needed to make it happen.

Hobbies. If one or both of you have "hobby stuff," take time to discuss where you will do your hobby and where you will keep your supplies. Your wife can't know you are bothered by her art supplies stacked on the coffee table unless you communicate about it. Your husband will continue to repair his mountain bike in the middle of the kitchen unless you come up with an alternative place. Discuss a plan for where you will keep your hobby stuff. While you are at it, take some time to talk about how much time you each will devote to your hobbies. Do you need to make your hobbies off-limits during certain times of the day or week in order to protect your marriage sanctuary? Write down your hobby plan along with any action steps necessary to make it happen.

Food for Thought: Sharing Hobbies. If you can find a hobby to share *together*, this can be a wonderful addition to your marriage sanctuary. Spending time together cooking, skiing, riding bikes, reading mystery novels, etc., is a great way to build your relationship. Eric and I enjoy taking black-and-white photos and creating artistic memory albums of our life together—many Sunday afternoons are spent printing and framing our latest photography masterpieces. Be on the look-out for things you both enjoy doing, and look for ways to build those activities into your marriage sanctuary. If there are any hobbies you plan to do together, write them down, along with any action steps needed to get started.

Work Stuff. If one or both of you have work stuff around the house—whether you work from home or bring projects home from your job—discuss where you are going to keep your work-related items. An intimate bedroom atmosphere can quickly be quelled by a stack of unfinished work sitting next to the bed. A fun evening together can be ruined by an open briefcase flooded with stressful work reminders. When it comes to your marriage sanctuary, it's vital to keep work in its proper place. Maybe you have decided to be home from the office by five every night to make your marriage a top pri-ority. But you can't be just physically home from work by five; you must be *mentally* and *emotionally* home from work in order to cultivate your marriage sanctuary. Work stuff lying around the house often serves only to remind you of your job and keep your mind distracted and worried. So if you must bring work-related things home, find a place for them where they will not hinder your precious time together.

Write down your plan for storing work stuff, along with any action steps necessary to make your plan work.

If you can think of other "stuff" in your home that is in need of a system, discuss it and write down your action plan.

Creating Your Ideal Home Atmosphere

Look back at the words that describe your ideal home atmosphere on page 172. Then spend some time discussing practical ways you can build your home atmosphere around the things that matter most to you. For example, if you desire an organized home, what are some things you can do to begin the organization process? Do you need to clean out your basement? Remove the clutter from your living room? Create a filing system for all those papers on your desk? If you desire a romantic home, what will help you build that environment? Do you need to get some candles? Make a CD of your favorite love songs? Creatively display pictures from your love story and/or wedding?

As mentioned earlier, Eric and I describe our ideal home environment as creative, organized, peaceful, and fun. Here are some examples of how we have built our home atmosphere around those things:

Creative. Instead of displaying pictures of fruit or watering cans on our walls, we display artistically framed black-and-white photos (many that we have taken ourselves) that have significant meaning to us. We love the environment of coffee shops, so we gave our kitchen a coffee-shop atmosphere, with bags of coffee beans and tea boxes on display, a collection of oversized coffee mugs, and pictures of our favorite coffee drinks on the walls. In our sitting room, where we often meet with other people, we decided to place four vintage-style club chairs in a circle instead of the typical couch and love seat. We have fun coming up with these creative ways to build our home. They are little things that may not mean much to anyone else, but to us they are unique expressions of our own personal marriage sanctuary.

Organized. Getting and staying organized isn't easy. It often takes years before a couple can master the art of maintaining an organized home. But Eric and I have found that it is well worth the effort. Being organized helps us function better in every area of life. Something that has greatly helped us in this process is to study the ways we each work best and organize our home accordingly. For example, Eric is a visual person. He does not like to keep important papers hidden away, out of his sight, such as in a filing cabinet. As a result, his desk would often be overflowing with papers that he "needed to keep in sight." So we customized an organization plan according to what would work for him. Instead of keeping his papers in file drawers or cabinets, we keep them out on his desk, in open storage boxes that are stacked and labeled. That way, he can see everything he is working on and still feel that his papers are organized rather than piled up on his desk.

Peaceful. One of the biggest things that robs from the peace of our home is clutter. It is hard for both of us to relax when the kitchen counter is littered with dishes and the hallway is overflowing with stuff from our last ski trip. So every morning we take fifteen minutes to pick up the house. That way, our messes never get out of control, and we begin our day with a peaceful, clean environment.

Fun. We have found that having the right kind of music in our house can contribute to a fun atmosphere. During dinner we often play jazz or swing music, and during our romantic evenings together we play our favorite love songs. We also have a digital camera that takes video clips, and throughout the month we film "snippets" of our daily life—we shoot fifteen-second clips of us having friends over for dinner, playing with our baby boy, even cleaning our garage. Every couple of months, we compile the video clips into a miniature family movie with fun background music. It helps us remember and appreciate the enjoyment we can find in everyday life.

Getting Specific

Things to Buy. For each idea that you write down, be sure to write a list of anything you need to buy before you can begin. Even if you don't have a lot of money to work with, there are many creative, low-cost or even free ways to build your ideal home environment. A marriage sanctuary isn't about the *things* in your home; it is about the *attitude* in your home.

The first year that Eric and I were married, we had barely enough money to cover the basics, let alone buy extras for our house. But we still desired to make our home into a romantic sanctuary. Eric's sister was keeping an old couch and a chair in storage. We asked if we could "store" them in our living room instead. Then we bought an inexpensive slipcover for the couch and put a matching pillow on the chair. Eric had an old trunk from his childhood that contained his stories and drawings from elementary school. We put a runner down the middle of it, set our wedding album on top of it, and made it into a coffee table. We decorated the living room with candles and picture frames that we'd been given as wedding gifts. We didn't have a kitchen table, so we covered a card table with a tablecloth and some flowers. We found a couple of old wooden chairs at a garage sale that had "character." For about fifty dollars total, we were able to create a wonderful home environment in which to begin building our marriage sanctuary.

If money is an issue, look at what you *do* have to work with and think of ways to use those things creatively. Do you have some old furniture that you could cover or refinish? Can you transform your bedroom by painting the walls a new color? Can you buy some candles for fifty cents apiece to create a romantic ambience? Sometimes, the challenge of making a great home environment out of odd pieces of this and that can be just as much fun as having a wad of money to spend on new furnishings and decorations.

Time Allotment. It's one thing to dream about creating your ideal home atmosphere, but to make it really happen you have to hollow out time to focus on it. For each idea that you have written down, discuss *when* you are going to implement it. Building your home environment may take more than just an hour or two. Consider blocking out a regular time each week to spend on building your home atmosphere, such as every Saturday morning or every Sunday afternoon. Write it on your calendar, if necessary. If you find it helpful, you can also write down the specific thing you are going to do during that time. This Saturday could be your day to "go to the paint store and look at paint samples," and next Saturday could be your day to "paint the bedroom."

Note: There may be goals in your home building plan that will take only one of you to accomplish. If you are more interested in decorating than your spouse, you don't need to force your spouse to sit and watch as you decide where to put the flower vase. It's okay to assign one person or the other certain projects in creating your home environment. The important thing is to agree together on what kind of home sanctuary you want to create and how you want to go about creating it. And the more you can do together, the more you will strengthen your teammate relationship with your spouse.

In a Nutshell

God's principle of sanctuary is simple: *Protect and preserve that which is most important.* In a marriage this principle is the key to unlocking lifelong romance. After all, what's most important in our married lives? Well, our relationships with God are supremely important, but after that, there should be nothing higher on our priority lists than . . . *each other.* And it's when we learn to truly value, cherish, and guard the position of this extraordinary relationship in our lives that we discover the fairy-tale enchantment of married love.

Urban myth states that romance disintegrates in marriage only moments after a couple arrive back from their honeymoon. This is simply not true. That is, it is not true for the couples who learn to protect sanctuary.

As a couple, you have a choice in how you will live out your married life together. You can have a lifestyle that reflects heaven's beauty, or you can have a lifestyle that showcases this world's crazed frenzy. Romance isn't cultivated in the midst of harried schedules, cluttered houses, and microwave dinners eaten hastily in front of *Seinfeld.* Romance doesn't thrive with exhausted husbands sacked out in the recliner in front of the nightly news and haggard wives chasing screaming kids around the house. True romance isn't the giving of a single daffodil, but the entire structuring of a life around order, beauty, simplicity, and serenity. True romance is a life full of daffodils.

The enchantment of marriage is found by those who know how to preserve the sacred meadowlands of their lives. The marriages that never lose the secret mountain alcoves will always be captivating. The marriages that never allow the glory of simple sunsets to lose their roseate luster will never cease to find fascination and delight in intimate love. The marriages that know how to protect and preserve that which matters most will bathe in the glories of lifelong romance.

To protect the sacred time and the sacred space in your life takes discipline. As a couple, you must become trained soldiers standing guard at the entry points to these priceless lands. Boundaries must be set in place to preserve the most important things in your life. These boundaries must be guarded and daily maintained. All distractions and hindrances to a healthy marriage must be eliminated. This takes watchfulness and an amazing amount of focused effort. Every word that you speak in public about your private life as a couple must be guarded and carefully monitored. Every activity or influence you allow into your home must be vigilantly examined. A sanctuary can be discovered only by a couple who take marriage intimacy seriously.

In living with a spouse, you can have merely a house in which you both reside, or you can create a marriage sanctuary in which your romance blossoms. You can have merely a bedroom in which you sleep, or you can have sacred space in which the smell of a million daffodils is in the air. You can have a lifestyle of chaos, stress, and the pursuit of money and fame, or you can have a life that exudes the order, beauty, simplicity, and serenity of heaven.

Epilogue

ARE YOU IN, OR ARE YOU OUT?

- Eric -

If you read chapter 1, then you know I wake up every morning with a desire to have the greatest marriage in the world. But I not only want to have the greatest marriage in the world; I want to be the greatest husband in the world, I want to have the best sex life any couple in all of world history has ever experienced, I want to be the most selfless servant-hearted man ever to walk this earth (outside of Christ, of course), and I want my home to be considered the number one marriage sanctuary on all of earth's surface.

In other words, I'm *not* aiming low.

But my question to you is, are you aiming low? When all is said and done, are you going to let me just prance on into heaven and receive all the above-mentioned accolades? Or are you going to put up a fight and scrap to have your name on the trophy instead of mine? Are you going to settle for an everyday, mediocre love saga, or are you willing to give everything for the cause of Christlikeness? Are you ready to compete at the Olympic level?

Are you in, or are you out?

There are a lot of seemingly worthy things to dedicate your life to these days. My college friend Chuck, for instance, is making his pitch to be selected to the Beer Belly Hall of Fame. And my coffee shop chum Andy is on the road to being the next great rock star who can't sing a lick. Oh, they are dedicated to their crafts, all right. But I don't consider either one of them competition when it comes to the championships of married love. Their energies are wrongly directed into things that really don't matter. And their marriages, to put it mildly, *stink*!

Where others aim to become the world's strongest human or the next apprentice to Donald Trump, are you willing to make having an extraordinary Christ-built marriage your ambition? Do you realize that the world around you will scoff at such a pursuit? From personal experience, I can assure you that not many will understand your efforts. The Chucks of the world will just burp their dismay, while the Andys of the world will sit down with their guitars and write very bad love songs about your perceived insanity.

I must forewarn you. Aiming for a great marriage is not only a lonely road—it also carries with it a hefty price tag. Amazing love doesn't come cheap. It will cost you everything. It will take your pride and flush it down the toilet; it will tax every millimeter of your soul and ruthlessly expose your every selfish tendency; it will renovate your entire existence.

So I ask you. *Are you in, or are you out?*

Remember, to compete at a world-class level in the arena

of love demands extreme dedication, the focus of your entire being, and a staggering expenditure of heart, mind, and body. This is certainly not life under a shade tree—it's an emotional, physical, and psychological obstacle course in which only the fortified survive.

Great marriages are the stuff of the heartiest and stoutest souls. They're boot camp for the entire inner life, the testing of the fiber of the heart, and the proving ground for the true substance of one's love. If you have Chuck-like pursuits or Andy-like ambitions that are greater than your longing for a great marriage, then you'll never cut it in the game of love. Your passion for God and for your spouse must take priority over selfish pursuits and ambitions. This isn't a side game of Indian poker we're playing here! This is serious stuff!

Is this really something that you want to do?

Every newly married spouse wants to have a great marriage, but as the months and years pass, the frauds are separated from the genuine lovers. The frauds were interested in the sparkle of marriage as long as it came easy, while the genuine lovers realized that amazing romance is something a couple must fight for, must sacrifice to obtain, and must be willing to give of themselves on a daily basis for an entire lifetime to preserve.

Even if you did achieve this extraordinary depth of intimacy in marriage, there will be no gold medal awaiting you on a podium in the end, no screaming crowd to applaud your many efforts, and no Wheaties-box photo op to authenticate your sacrifice for posterity. No one outside your God, your spouse, and your children may ever know what you have achieved. If you are craving recognition, this isn't the path for you. And if you are interested in the cheering crowd, then there are much more self-glorifying pursuits on which to spend your life.

So I'll ask you one more time, *Are you in, or are you out?*

For Those Who Are In

Leslie and I would like those of you who are "in" to know that we are thrilled to have you as competition in the upcoming years. The thrill of marriage only increases when you realize that others are attempting to outdo you.

But the most important thing we want you to know is that you will certainly never regret your decision. Creating a great marriage may be the most difficult thing you ever do, but it will also be the best thing you ever do.

I know it sounds fun to stand on an Olympic podium with a gold medal around your neck and act like you're singing your national anthem for a billion eyes to see, but a great marriage is even better. The reward for great love is even more amazing, and so much more satisfying. Great love wins the applause of heaven, the utter delight and total affection of your spouse for a lifetime, the purest and most perfect intimate pleasure a human can possibly know, and as a final bonus, the lifelong admiration and respect of your children.

A great marriage is the purest, most fantastic, most exhilarating, most satisfying pleasure a human could possibly know this side of heaven. It is rich with intimacy, stockpiled with laughter, overflowing with affection, and jam-packed with the countless joys of a shared existence with another life.

It's true that a great marriage may cost you everything, but what it costs doesn't even compare to the payout. A great marriage gives back ten thousand times more than it takes. And it is worth every effort, every bead of sweat, and every painful moment of sacrifice needed in order to discover it.

A great marriage designed and built by Christ turns ordinary sappy romantics into extraordinary superheroic spouses. It builds an inner tensile strength strong enough to break through even the toughest steel walls life can place in front of us. A great marriage orchestrated by God effervesces with the most perfect and exhilarating sexual pleasure, uniting two individuals into a most extraordinary human team. And it brings about a truly enchanting lifestyle loaded with romance and supernatural beauty.

Leslie and I are convinced that we have the most beautiful romance on planet Earth. Of course, we are biased. And it's very likely if you allow Jesus Christ to script your love story that you too may feel that you have it better than anyone else in all the world. That's just God's way.

When it's all said and done, we won't be the ones standing on that podium in heaven anyway. This love story is not about *our* romantic prowess; it's all about *His*. He is the true Prince Charming. And in the end, we'll be throwing our crowns at our heavenly Lover's feet, proclaiming Him to be the One responsible for every good thing that ever took place in our lives.

Here's to the kind of happily ever after that lasts for all eternity!

NOTES

Chapter One: How to Have the Perfect Marriage

1. Leslie and I write about developing this lifestyle in great detail in our book *When God Writes Your Life Story: Experience the Ultimate Adventure* (Sisters, OR: Multnomah, 2004).

Chapter Two: How to Stay Madly in Love Through Life's Ups and Downs

1. The Voice of the Martyrs, *Hearts of Fire* (Nashville: W Publishing, 2003), 110.

Chapter Three: How to Have an Extraordinary Sex Life

1. Eric Ludy and Leslie Ludy, *When Dreams Come True: A Love Story Only God Could Write* (Sisters, OR: Multnomah, 2004).

2. Eric Ludy, *God's Gift to Women: Discovering the Lost Greatness of Masculinity* (Sisters, OR: Multnomah, 2003).

3. Joshua Harris, *Not Even a Hint: Guarding Your Heart Against Lust* (Sisters, OR: Multnomah, 2003).

Chapter Four: How to Tackle Life as a Team

1. Howard G. Hendricks and William D. Hendricks, *Living by the Book* (Chicago: Moody, 1993).

2. Eric Ludy, *God's Gift to Women.*

Chapter Five: How to Build the Ultimate Romantic Sanctuary

1. Corie ten Boom, John and Elizabeth Sherrill, *The Hiding Place,* (Uhrichsville, OH, Barbour and Company, Inc.), 150.

93735